Teaching Notes on Piano Exam Pieces 2015 & 2016

Grades 1–7

TIMOTHY BARRATT
SHARON GOULD
JULIAN HELLABY
MARGARET MURRAY McLEOD
ANTHONY WILLIAMS

Teaching Notes on Piano Exam Pieces 2015 & 2016

Grades 1–7

With an introduction by JOHN HOLMES, Chief Examiner

ABRSM

First published in 2014 by
ABRSM (Publishing) Ltd, a wholly owned subsidary of ABRSM

© 2014 by The Associated Board of the Royal Schools of Music

ISBN: 978 1 84849 673 6

AB 3778

A CIP catalogue for this book is available from The British Library.

Cover by Kate Benjamin & Andy Potts
Typeset by Hope Services (Abingdon) Ltd
Printed in England by Caligraving Ltd, Thetford, Norfolk

FSC
www.fsc.org

MIX
Paper from
responsible sources
FSC™ C109619

CONTENTS

NOTES ON CONTRIBUTORS

Timothy Barratt, ARAM GRSM LRAM ARCM LMusTCL, studied at the RAM and in Paris with Vlado Perlemuter. A solo pianist, accompanist and chamber music player, he also has considerable experience of teaching at all levels. Previously a lecturer and vocal coach at the RAM and Trinity College of Music, he is now Head of Keyboard at Dulwich College. He is an ABRSM examiner, trainer, consultant moderator and presenter, and a mentor for the Certificate of Teaching course.

Sharon Gould, MA ARCM, read music at Cambridge University, and has performed extensively as a harpsichord soloist and Baroque orchestral director in the UK and internationally. She is also a piano accompanist and chamber musician. She has taught at the RCM Junior Department, at Chetham's School of Music and at the RNCM; her former students include several international award winners. She has been an ABRSM examiner since 2003 and joined the training panel in 2008.

Julian Hellaby, PhD MMus BMus LRAM ARAM, studied piano at the RAM and has performed throughout the UK and overseas. He is an ABRSM examiner, trainer, moderator and public presenter, as well as a mentor for the Certificate of Teaching course. He has extensive experience of piano teaching at all levels, and is currently Associate Research Fellow at Coventry University. He has released six CDs, and his book *Reading Musical Interpretation* was published by Ashgate in 2009.

Margaret Murray McLeod, ARAM FTCL LRAM ARCM, studied piano and composition at the RAM. As well as performing as a soloist and accompanist, she has many years' experience of teaching at all levels. From 1972 she trained student teachers and performers at Edinburgh Napier University, where she was Senior Lecturer for Performance Studies until 1997. Her work as a lecturer, examiner and adjudicator has taken her worldwide.

Anthony Williams, MMus Dip.RAM GRSM LRAM, has an active performing, teaching and adjudicating career in the UK and abroad and is currently Head of Keyboard and Instrumental Music at Radley College, Oxfordshire. As a piano specialist he regularly presents teacher support lecture-recitals and is an examiner (jazz and classical), trainer and moderator for ABRSM. He is the compiler of *Fingerprints* and the *Best of Grade* series for piano, and editor of *Simply Classics* (all published by Faber Music).

INTRODUCTION

Choosing new pieces is always exciting – rather like setting out on a journey to somewhere you haven't been before. As a teacher, you are presented with an opportunity to match your students' skills and preferences to the right music for them, while also making use of your expertise to ensure the right level of challenge to encourage the development of technique and musicianship. This book is intended to help guide you in making good decisions, together with your student, about which pieces will work most successfully. It sets out to provide useful insights into each piece, which we hope will support you and your students on your teaching and learning journeys.

The expert contributors are all experienced teachers and ABRSM examiners. They are able to draw from their knowledge and understanding gained in each of these contexts to provide valuable hints and tips, as well as helpful advice on how to develop the musical relationship which links composer, score and performer.

In fact, the choice of piece is only the first in an almost never-ending series of choices which becomes the learning journey I mentioned at the beginning. Whether it's Bach, Beethoven or Bartók, Telemann, Tansman or Turina, a whole range of decisions – conscious and subconscious – will need to be made in order for the developing pianist to arrive at their destination, in this case, the exam performance. Tempo, touch, fingering, pedalling, phrasing... the list of choices goes on, so perhaps it would be helpful here to talk about how the decision-making process might be approached.

It is crucial to note that there is no 'ABRSM way' of playing any of our piano exam pieces, although of course there *is* an 'ABRSM way' of assessing how they are played. This is by considering the overall musical outcome – in effect, the cumulative result of all the various musical and technical decisions that will have been made in preparing the performance. For example, ABRSM examiners don't assess fingering, but we do comment on and evaluate its effects, such as evenness of tone or regularity of delivery, which are so often partly the result of fingering choices. Examiners are listening and looking for the degree of skill a candidate shows in controlling elements of pitch, time, tone, shape and performance, which develop gradually during their learning and practice prior to the

1

exam. It is these elements which form the basis of our marking criteria, which are used by examiners in all ABRSM practical graded exams.

As musicians we are often presented with a range of sources, and it can sometimes be a puzzle to establish what 'truth' about each piece really is. In this case we have the printed scores, the ABRSM recordings and these *Teaching Notes*. There is truth in all these sources; each presents a different perspective on the same thing. The scores provide a notated record of what was written by the composer and later published in the ABRSM edition, the recordings present realized performances of the music and the *Teaching Notes* add various ideas relating to interpretation. There may well be differences between what the scores imply, what the recordings present and what these *Teaching Notes* recommend – but in reality they do not so much contradict as complement each other.

That's the excitement of every musical journey – there will always be a variety of routes to a successful musical result, and our examiners do not mark candidates according to any particular one; instead they judge the combined effectiveness of the various musical performance decisions you and your student have made, taken as a whole. This means that every candidate can play to their strengths, not only in their particular choice of pieces, but also in the way that they interpret them. For example, there is a range of tempos – a 'bandwidth' of speeds – at which any given piece can successfully be played. For some pieces this will be wider than for others, but even where a metronome mark is given, there is usually room for some flexibility of approach. The examiner will not be marking the speed of playing absolutely or in isolation, but rather in conjunction with other elements of performance, such as note accuracy and rhythmic character. The right tempo choice for each student is best determined as part of a comfortable balance between this and other elements, so that one element is not sacrificed to another – precision sacrificed to speed, for example.

Between them, the ABRSM scores, recordings and *Teaching Notes* are intended to open a variety of doorways to interpretation. Although these publications are the result of considerable research, drawn from contributors with a wealth of experience, none of our resources can portray and communicate everything within the music. We would like to encourage you to inspire your students to play with creativity and individuality, leading them to achieve successful performances that suit and reflect their particular skills, strengths and enthusiasms. In effect, there needs to be a collaborative partnership between you and each of your students, as they learn how best to portray the composer's musical ideas in their own personal way.

Right through from Grade 1 to Grade 8, each list of pieces, A, B and C, will tend to prioritize certain aspects of piano playing by focusing broadly upon a particular style or group of styles:

List A contains music which generally calls for emphasis on definition of finger-work, clarity of articulation, control of co-ordination, management of texture and (often) ornaments. Part-playing will often feature in List A at the higher grades, where the skill of balancing the various lines of separate voices effectively will be brought under the spotlight.

List B pieces are particularly likely to call for tonal warmth, expressive musical shaping, sensitive phrasing and a sense of melody, since they are mostly in Classical and Romantic styles. Cantabile tone will be needed for melodic lines here, as a feeling for phrase structure becomes more central to a convincing performance. Pedalling will be necessary for many of these works, especially those requiring legato effects and richer sonorities. As with so many other aspects of piano playing, there is no single right way to approach pedalling. Its effect on tone and shape will be taken into account by examiners, but they will be assessing the effect of pedalling on the over-all musical outcome, rather than the strict observance of any printed pedal indications. This means that these may be adapted or omitted to suit the needs of the individual, although pieces whose full musical effect is heav-ily reliant on pedalling (whether marked in the music or not) should be avoided, if appropriate pedalling cannot be managed. As the grades pro-gress, List B pieces often also call for an ability to manage tempo with a greater degree of flexibility, leading eventually to the need for balanced rubato – musical 'give and take' within the basic pulse. The musical mood and personality of List B pieces will also highlight the candidate's ability to control dynamic changes smoothly and, especially at more advanced grades, to mould and colour the tone in order to realize the necessary stylistic characteristics.

List C offers the widest range of styles, and here there is ample opportun-ity to find something to suit every student. You will find this especially by exploring the many pieces that are not published in the selected volumes. The pieces, which often involve jazzy rhythms and harmonies, can be particularly appealing to students, and therefore a strong motivation to practise! List C pieces will tend to emphasize subtleties of touch, idiom-atic inflections and embellishments, but perhaps above all, the need to project a clear sense of musical identity and character. Quite often here the scope for interpretive decisions is considerable: straight or swing quavers, for example. Once again there is no single right way to play these pieces, and the best result will arise from a well-judged match between each individual candidate's piano skills, and the particular demands of the chosen piece.

It is worth reiterating that using the ABRSM marking criteria (which can be found online and within the piano syllabus), examiners will assess the musical outcome heard on the day: the musical effectiveness of the piano playing in the exam room. Live music-making is at the heart of ABRSM's approach and underlying philosophy.

Candidates can choose the order in which they play their three pieces, and whether to start the exam with these or another section – scales, for example. Once again there is no single right way; as with so much of the musical learning journey leading up to the performance, the exam itself starts with a decision!

We do hope that you will feel excited and inspired by the huge range of musical possibilities open to you and your students within the 2015 & 2016 ABRSM Piano syllabus. Spanning around 400 years of composition, whether it's Dussek or Debussy, there is truly something for everyone to embark upon and enjoy.

John Holmes

GRADE 1

Students will usually have been learning for up to 18 months by the time Grade 1 is on the horizon. They may have taken the Prep Test during this time, in which case they will probably feel quite confident when facing their first graded exam. A wide choice of pieces should help to keep motivation high, so why not have some alternatives prepared, then choose the best three as the exam approaches? You can find the marking criteria for all grades in the 2015 & 2016 ABRSM Piano syllabus and on our website.

A:1 Clementi *Arietta*

The title Arietta, meaning 'Little Song', gives the clue to the character of this charming piece, with its clear phrase shape and singable melody. The notes should present few problems since there are no awkward changes of hand-position. The main challenge is to create a gentle mood with well-shaped cantabile lines accompanied by a less prominent left hand.

The main consideration in tempo choice is that the music should flow easily in crotchet beats. A constant pulse should be maintained when the quavers switch hands at bar 8, and the tendency to hurry at the final *forte* must be avoided. Phrases are usually four bars in length and a slight breath at the end of each one will help to punctuate the piece.

The characteristic 'sighing' appoggiatura, first heard in bar 2, becomes a feature throughout the piece. A little stress on the first note, followed by a gently released second note, will produce the desired graceful effect. Clear rests, released exactly on the second crotchet, will let air into the texture at bars 8–10. The rise in pitch in these bars seems to suggest a crescendo, to be reversed as the hairpins that follow effect a diminuendo for the return to *piano*. The two left-hand B♭s add colour to the otherwise purely diatonic C major and the *forte* at bar 17 provides a welcome surprise for the ending.

A:2 Haydn *Minuet in G*

The majestic, stately mood of this dance seems to evoke perfectly the atmosphere of an eighteenth-century candlelit ballroom. Imagine a scene of sumptuously dressed people enjoying the elegant movements of a minuet to music provided by a resident orchestra.

The tempo should have an unhurried feel, with a mixture of strong and weaker beats giving definition to the dance steps. Phrasing is largely left to individual choice: either detaching all crotchets or incorporating some slurs, while sustaining the remaining notes, are both stylish options. Left-hand leaps may need individual practice, especially where the fifth finger needs to move up an octave without hesitation at the double bar, and in the right hand a few slight finger twists might trip up a less secure candidate.

A strong, confident tone, with secure fingerwork, immediately establishes the character. Tapering of the quavers in bar 3 will prepare the way for a sufficiently gentle *piano*; this in turn allows an exciting yet carefully graded and rhythmically poised crescendo as the music approaches the midway cadence in D major.

The second half follows a similar musical pattern. You may prefer to drop below *mezzo-forte* in order to provide greater scope for the crescendo. A well-paced ritardando through the final quaver group and a full-length final note will ensure that an elegant composure remains to the end of the performance.

A:3 Trad. English, arr. Davies
The Lincolnshire Poacher

The inclusion of well-crafted arrangements is by now a familiar feature of the piano syllabus. The rollicking tune, together with the tempo changes and quirky harmonic touches, gives this lively piece an instant appeal.

Establishing the optimum tempo is often a challenge for inexperienced players, especially when exam nerves tend to get in the way. The natural stress and lilt of the two-in-a-bar pulse can be felt by singing the melody, with or without the words. The slurs from the weak to strong parts of the beat form a major musical feature throughout the piece; special practice, perhaps using a scale or five-finger pattern, will help to define the separation of each two-note figure. The left-hand role is mainly to accompany, playing either smooth legato lines or more detached chords. Careful listening will ensure that all chord-notes sound evenly, especially the fifth finger, and confident co-ordination is needed for the independent phrasing in bars 3–4.

The dynamic contrasts can be enhanced if the *mezzo-forte* phrases drop further in volume. The crescendo and ritardando in bars 11–12 that lead to the pause on the augmented chord and the tempo changes in the final four bars help add touches of humour to a performance; this is particularly effective when followed by a light ending, played as quickly as is safe to do so.

A:4 Blow *Hornpipe*

This cheerful, energetic hornpipe will prove a good choice for a student with strong fingers and the confidence to sustain fast running notes. The spring in its step seems to evoke perfectly the scene of a sailors' lively dance, designed to stave off cold winds and boredom while on board ship.

The tricky twists and turns in the right-hand fingerwork will govern the choice of tempo. Plenty of right-hand practice, using reliable, consistent fingering, will ensure fluency. Individually tailored exercises based on the B–F♯ right-hand position in bars 5–7 will develop control of the fifth finger. Unwanted accents can be avoided in the final run by smooth thumb turns.

Feeling two, not four, beats in a bar is the key to creating a rhythmic energy, which is not weighed down by unwanted accents. Crisply articulated quavers, evenly paced and with no audible overlap of sounds, will give a definition to the melodic shape. The printed slurs, when sensitively tapered, add an elegant touch at cadences. The detached crotchets elsewhere, neatly co-ordinated with the left hand, will provide some seafaring buoyancy.

A firm *forte* start will immediately capture the rousing mood. In other places you might experiment with quieter dynamic levels, especially at the start of the final crescendo, always tracing the natural rise and fall of each phrase.

A:5 L. Mozart *Menuett in G*

Although this piece is a minuet with the same key as A:2 in the Grade 1 syllabus its character is quite different. The scalic right-hand lines, accompanied alternately by chords and single notes, call for sensitive shaping, and the virtually blank musical canvas provides players with the opportunity to explore their own ideas.

Each half follows a similar musical pattern of two two-bar phrases followed by one of four bars. The opening two-bar phrase suggests a gentle crescendo towards the start of the second bar. Care will be needed to synchronize legato quavers with detached chords, and a bump on the final thumb note should be avoided. The repeated left-hand Gs serve to reinforce the tonic; using the tip of the fingers will ensure that all chord notes sound evenly.

The clear contours of the longer arching phrase encourage a corresponding rise and fall in tone. Dropping back to *piano* at bar 5 allows an effective crescendo, and the final appoggiatura, with its harmonic clash and subsequent release of tension, needs sensitive handling. Reliable fingering will prevent the right-hand quavers from faltering; teaching a chromatic scale will help secure the semitone pattern. Various phrasing options for the accompanying crotchets may be explored; a mixture of slurs and detached notes will work particularly well. Finally, a confident two-octave left-hand leap will guarantee that momentum is not held up at the halfway point.

A:6 Neefe *Allegretto in C*

Confident dynamics and a feel for phrase-shaping are the key ingredients for a musical performance of this beautiful, song-like piece. The notes are fairly straightforward, with most activity confined to the right hand, and the Allegretto marking suggests a gentle unhurried flow.

The opening section, repeated identically at the end of the piece, is constructed of two two-bar phrases followed by one of four bars, each with the defining feature of a detached first right-hand quaver and an appoggiatura to finish. Gently detaching the end of each two-bar phrase will allow the music to breathe. Well-contrasted dynamic levels and a shapely end of phrase will create the necessary grace and elegance. In the longer phrase, which completes the section, the shape of the note-patterns seems to determine the rise and fall of tone. An ornament in the penultimate bar is optional. An even triplet rhythm would work well for the three notes of the mordent; if this decorative feature is included, it must not hinder the musical flow.

The central section, with its more continuous sequential quaver movement, suggests one unbroken musical line. Dynamic contrasts fall into two-bar blocks at the start, calling for subtle dynamic shading in order to achieve a smooth blend between *forte* and *piano*. The semiquavers in bar 15 need careful pacing and clear fingerwork and, as always, no hesitation should interrupt the flow between sections.

B:1 Gurlitt *Das Schaukelpferd (The Rocking Horse)*

Horses, real or pretend, have inspired a diverse range of children's piano pieces from Schytte to Schumann, and the latter's 'Ritter vom Steckenpferd' from *Kinderszenen* is particularly worth comparing. Gurlitt combines elements of Schumann's wild abandon with a 'hunting horn' motif in the opening figures, making no secret of where we imagine we are.

Conveying the horse's rocking is important to communicating the energy and excitement of the ride. The one-in-a-bar feel suggests a fast tempo; a firm emphasis at the start of bar 1 and a lighter emphasis at the start of bar 2 will give the impression of the leap forwards followed by the more relaxed backwards swing. The staccato anacrusis avoids the initial impetus becoming too forceful.

Dynamically the opening eight bars are all one phrase; a slight crescendo to bar 5 works well before dying away a little. This will help highlight the *forte* in the next phrase – a sudden dramatic and galloping A minor scale. These bars need a firm tone and rhythmic emphasis, which will add excitement; the tied E must be full-length – an abrupt lull in the rocking before the fading echo in the *poco rit.*

The opening returns, but this time there might be a sudden *piano* in bar 18 followed by a crescendo to the final dotted crotchet, as our imaginary horse prepares to leap the largest fence of all before heading off across the fields.

B:2 Knut Nystedt *Løvet faller (Falling Leaves)*

This piece may not only reflect falling leaves but also express a tinge of sadness that the dark, cold Norwegian winter is around the corner.

The suggested tempo conveys the gentle rocking drop of the leaves as they fall and is on the cusp of one in a bar. Feeling this across two bars (as if in 6/4 time) will give a lovely lightness and delicate end to the opening phrases. The excellent left-hand fingering will avoid any hesitation.

From bar 5 a longer four-bar phrase implies a breath of wind, but a slight flutter of the leaf is all that is needed as the phrase swells with the gentlest of crescendos. A lift after the first crotchet in bar 7 will provide the light touch required for the repeated notes.

Bars 9 to 12 move optimistically to the relative major, like sunshine warming up the red and golden leaves. The *mf* should not be too robust, needing simply a little more projection of the melodic line, with greater weight behind the right-hand fingers to carry the tune. Achieving the right balance between hands is crucial even in early grades and makes a huge, musical difference to the interpretation.

The smallest of ritardandos in bar 14 will give the leaf a soft landing, and a tiny breath before the delicate final chords will provide a moment of repose as the leaf settles on to the ground.

B:3 Trad. Catalan, arr. Marshall *El cant dels ocells (The Song of the Birds)*

For the imaginative pianist this piece is a gift; the song, bird-call and sound-world are evocative and entrancing. The title reveals everything about the colours and tempo, and detailed expressive markings guide the performer.

The musical challenges of the opening lie in creating a controlled and singing legato line, the sounds overlapped with enough weight to produce a vocal tone but with a gentle, expressive crescendo. The tone needs to be sustained through bar 2 and relaxed in the second part of the phrase without angularity or interruption from the left-hand accompaniment.

The *rit.* in bar 6 is best achieved by thinking in quavers, maintaining the slowing pulse through the minim and pause bar while relishing the atmosphere produced by the pedal. Putting the pedal down early would catch notes from the first half of the bar, so this should be avoided; the sounds finally lift for the breath (comma in bar 7) before the song resumes. Subtle control of the sound is required in bar 9 where the left-hand C could become intrusive, and bar 13 needs a sense of the melody going to the left hand's A.

The held left-hand 3rds and the pedalled effect across the right-hand motifs in the final bars are gorgeous. Lifting the pedal after the following 3rd sounds will avoid too abrupt an end to the beautiful bird-call; this will help the right-hand crotchet extend a little across the bar-line.

B:4 Gedike *Heiteres Lied (Cheerful Song)*

The cheerful melody, reminiscent of whistling on the way to work (or school) on a sunny morning, lives up to the title. The music's personality is underpinned by the delicate, guitar-like chordal accompaniment and an understated character.

The opening bar needs clarity of tone and articulation while keeping the staccato quavers light. The semiquavers that follow should be smooth and even, under control and legato yet musically shaped with a crescendo towards the middle of the bar.

The left hand's accompanying crotchet chords could easily obscure the charm of the tune and sound rather flat-footed, so they need a gentle lightness of touch and can be a slightly shorter chord than marked. Saving the full-length crotchet for the G in bar 4 enables an emphasis without too abrupt a tone. An appropriate tempo will help the jaunty feel, and conducting or walking two in a bar while singing the melody gives a good guide.

Dynamically, the small crescendo in bars 7 to 8 should be gently conveyed to the listener, saving a more pronounced crescendo and perhaps just the hint of a ritardando for bar 14. Here the music's predictable and simple nature is interrupted by a rather cheeky joke (a diminished 7th) before the walker carries on with a smile.

B:5 Lajos Papp *Waltz*

This is a hauntingly beautiful waltz, its melancholy and mysterious character conveyed by the Aeolian (or natural minor) scale and the delicacy of the accompaniment.

The melody sits comfortably under a five-finger hand-position and moves almost exclusively in step; the technical challenges all lie in the balance and subtlety of tonal control.

A tempo that is flowing yet unhurried is best achieved by singing the quavers later in the piece. The opening left-hand melody needs a smooth legato and a cellistic tone, with your student paying attention to the overlap of the sound; a natural dynamic rise and fall will follow the pitch contours. The accompanying chords should sound like lightly bowed violins – not plucked but gently detached, and so light as not to disturb the singing quality of the dotted minims. Judging the sound of the second chord in particular may require practice and will need a relaxed wrist, delicacy of touch and a gentle, tactile relationship with the key surface.

The few dynamics marked offer a golden opportunity to explore some additional contrasts, in order to show the musical direction and convey the story – perhaps save the softest moment for the last two bars. The staccato right-hand crotchet in the penultimate bar should not be abrupt but just a gentle lift before the listener is guided towards the tender A major chord at the end.

B:6 Ponchielli *Dance of the Hours*

'Hours' of fun can be had listening to versions of this popular dance, from the Act 3 Finale of the opera *La Gioconda*. For younger pianists the best introduction is in Disney's *Fantasia*, which conveys the appropriate playfulness and imagery.

The articulation works well, if interpreted within a musical context: a very short, unvaried staccato would put abrupt emphasis on offbeat quavers. The markings signal not just a detached note but also lightness at the end of couplets, achieved with a drop and lift of the hand, and a gentle crescendo to each bar's first beat. Two-beat phrases should be heard as part of the longer eight-bar melody, moving forwards and growing dynamically to the *mezzo-forte* and *poco rit.*

The left hand also needs delicacy and gentle control; after an important first note, the crotchets should lighten towards the middle of the bar. Again, a fall and rise of the hand will help this.

The tempo's playfulness and the dynamic shading will bring the piece to life. Your student might experiment with a cheeky hesitancy over the first two quavers before establishing a jaunty dance-like tempo (which at the *a tempo* might be a touch faster). Even at *piano* there should be a dynamic rise and fall across the two-bar phrases; the most convincing *mezzo-forte* should be saved for the melody's highest note, in bars 12–13, before a light throwaway end.

C:1 Stephen Clarke *The Giant's Coming*

Children always enjoy a scary story (as indeed do grown-ups!), so this will be a popular choice for players of all ages.

Distant rumblings herald the approach of the giant, and at first the accents should not be too loud but instead fit within the *pianissimo* level. If all the dynamics and accents are scrupulously observed your student will create an exciting scene.

For the right hand in bars 3–6 some players might prefer to place finger 2 on the A♮ of the triplets. This will then allow the thumb to make the A♭ accents and avoid a finger change in bar 6. Stronger fingering may also result from placing the thumb on the first quaver in bars 8 and 10.

The inclusion of the 5/4 bars gives a jolt to the rhythm, especially the second one (bar 6), which must be counted carefully. For the notes just before the pause it might be helpful to think of a whispered warning 'Look out!'. The excitement builds with the change to triple time and gradual crescendo, until the giant arrives in bars 12–14. The sudden *pianissimo* (bar 14) and the whole-bar pause that follows must not be overlooked. Everyone has run away, and the giant is left alone wondering, rather sadly, why nobody wanted to play with him.

C:2 Stephen Duro *Calypso Joe*

The West Indian calypso, with its syncopated rhythms and jaunty style, has a universal appeal. It conjures up pictures of white sands, hot sun and the wonderfully clear waters of the Caribbean.

The two main stresses of each bar lie on the first beat and the second half of the second beat. However, these should not be laboured – just felt as an easy but unequal swaying movement. The slur from quaver to crotchet (bar 2 and similar) should be treated like any other slur, with a down–up movement of the hand. This will make the crotchet quieter, and allow a tiny break in the sound before the hand drops into the following tied quaver.

Finger-changing on the first three notes is well worth practising, and should be matched with fingers 2-1-2 in bar 3. The left-hand part is very straightforward, lying comfortably under the five fingers (F–C) until a shift of hand-position in bar 14 for the last phrase.

Unless more dynamic variety is added, there will be very little contrast, especially when played without repeats. It should begin *forte* but at bar 5 it could change to *mezzo-forte*. Starting the second half *forte*, your student could make a stepwise decrescendo through the sequences to reach *mezzo-piano* at bar 13. Then a strong crescendo to *forte* for the last two bars will provide an exhilarating ending.

C:3 Eben *Na krmítku (Bird at the Feeding Box)*

Anyone who has a bird-table in their garden or who has watched birds feeding in the park will enjoy this delightfully descriptive piece. Teachers will also be pleased with the simple consistency of the fingering.

A light hand (wrist) staccato using a minimum of movement will imitate the quick, almost nervous effect of the pecking beaks. A little practice on a flat surface will create a crisp tapping sound that can then be transferred to the keyboard. The left hand provides a quiet, smooth background and should be played as legato as possible; all the fingering is provided to achieve this result.

One could imagine some jostling for position and ruffling of feathers from bar 6 when the music makes a crescendo and the left hand, with its squawking augmented 4ths, becomes more active. Care will be needed here to keep the hands co-ordinated while managing the different articulations. The dominant bird wins and resumes its pecking unchallenged (bar 10) until there is a querulous remark from the other contender in the penultimate bar. Without hurrying in the last two bars, your student should glide gently into the last chord, keeping the right hand very legato.

The suggested metronome mark does not pose any great demands, and the spacing-out of the ending rounds off the piece with no need of a rallentando.

C:4 Bartók *Children at Play*

Bartók composed some wonderful music for young players, and this set of folk-inspired pieces is a valuable part of the repertoire. However, as with all of Bartók's music, there are technical and musical challenges to be met.

The principal hurdle here is managing conflicting articulations. Often one hand plays staccato while the other plays legato or slurs. It is also important to notice the different types of articulation. As well as staccato, accents, two-note slurs and longer legato slurs, there are tenuto lines seen over many of the crotchets. These should be weighted down and held almost for their full duration.

This Hungarian melody is based on a children's handkerchief game. The nonsense words of the song – 'let's bake something – a snail strudel, round and sweet!' – indicate a mood of merriment. Plenty of practice with each hand alone will help to establish the correct articulation and attack. Once hands are together, the first section should not be difficult because the left hand is always legato. The second tune (bars 9–16) becomes trickier, especially as it builds to the climax at bar 13. Slow practice and careful listening will be essential.

Bartók was always very precise about metronome marks, and luckily this one is not unduly fast. Once the piece is thoroughly learnt, it would be fun to see if the performance is anywhere near the 32 seconds that the composer expects!

C:5 Ornstein *My, what a din the cuckoos are making!*

At first glance one might wonder why the two cuckoos in this exciting composition are singing perfect 4ths instead of the expected minor 3rd! In fact, as the old rhyme tells us, the cuckoo's call varies from month to month. ('Cuckoo, cuckoo, what do you do? / In April I open my bill; / In May I sing all day; / In June I change my tune…')

The familiar cuckoo of Daquin (and of many other composers) does sing a minor 3rd, but Beethoven's sings a major 3rd in the 'Pastoral' Symphony.

The piece should paint a colourful picture and it provides an excellent opportunity for developing staccato. Contrasts between the dynamics and the different articulations should be very positive. The two cuckoos seem to be competing with each other. The first is strong but the second (with accents) is the more aggressive. In the middle section the first one tries to chase the other away; starting very quietly, it gets more frantic as the tempo increases.

Some players may like to try the following fingering for the rising sequence beginning in bar 9. Left hand 1-5 on B/E then 2-4 on C/A; right hand 3-1 on G♯/E and 2-4 on A/C; this fingering will work until arriving at bar 16. The third section is exactly like the first, but should fade away to almost nothing. Have they both flown away?

C:6 Kevin Wooding *The House on the Hill*

This piece conjures up a haunted house on the hill, in a sinister, remote setting. Marked to be played 'terrifyingly', clearly something blood-curdling must have happened. This is a winner for the extrovert student who enjoys some dramatic fun at the piano!

A really crisp staccato is needed, with accents firmly marked. Apart from the occasional legato notes in the melody while the left hand remains stac-cato, there are few technical problems with which to grapple. It will be important to observe the quieter bars in order to highlight the more sinister moments such as the chromatic figures from bar 9 and the fear-some ending.

A metronome mark of minim = *c.*80 will give enough pace to create excitement without being dangerously precipitous. Counting should not be hurried as the climax is approached, and the listener must be made to wait for the massive low D that marks the *coup de grâce*! If the pedal is depressed at the very same moment it will create a more dramatic effect. Your student may enjoy using the thumb, or thumb and third finger, to play this note, if it can be reached comfortably. As the pedal is held throughout the last three bars, full arm weight can be dropped into each note. This will produce big tone without harshness, and make an impressive finish.

GRADE 2

Students may want to play something similar to their favourite piece from their Grade 1 exam, but there is plenty of choice, so do consider all the options both within and beyond ABRSM's books of exam pieces.

A:1 Handel *Impertinence*

The unusual title of this lovely piece is sure to stimulate some discussion between student and teacher. Maybe it is to do with the construction of the piece? At first it sounds as though it is going to be a straightforward canon, with both voices in agreement, but the bass is always a little different, as though interrupting and contradicting the first voice.

It will require a well-developed independence of the hands, so practice with each hand separately is advisable at first. For instance, in the first four bars of each section the two-bar phrases have a natural rise and fall in tone. This means that one hand will be making a slight crescendo while the other a diminuendo.

In view of the lively nature of the music, many of the crotchets could be played staccato. Some articulation marks have been suggested, but there is scope for individual decisions. It is usual, though, to detach upbeats in order to give emphasis to first-beat notes, and there must be a consistency in sequences and imitation.

The ornament (triplet quavers) in the penultimate bar of each section will sound pedantic at first, but once the music begins to flow at or near the suggested metronome speed, it will sound perfectly convincing. The piece should definitely dance along as two in a bar.

A:2 Schale *Minuet in C*

The character of this Minuet, by the little-known composer C. F. Schale, is elegant and affectionate. It captures the atmosphere of the court and gracious manners of the eighteenth century.

Much of the left-hand part could be lightly detached, with the rising quaver figures in bars 2 and 4 actually staccato; this is not only stylish, but aids facility, especially for the smaller hand. For contrast, the quavers in bars 10 and 12 could be legato.

The melody itself will require a warm singing tone; imagining a duet between flute and cello may help to find the correct balance between the hands. The right hand will be mostly legato. In the first half, the four-bar phrases should have a gently rising nuance to the middle of the phrase and then fall away towards the cadence to form a graceful arch. The slur in bar 6 (and similar) is in effect a tie to the first note of the short trill and is executed as shown above the bar.

The second half begins with two-bar phrases and is then balanced by one of four. Here the terraced dynamics marked in the score help to outline the shape of the phrasing; but your student should be sure to round off the last two bars with a diminuendo and, if liked, a slight rallentando.

A:3 Vanhal *Cantabile*

The length of this charming movement may deter some students from choosing it. However, as there is a certain amount of repetition, there are only 16 bars to learn in the right hand and the left hand has even fewer.

Marked *dolce*, it should begin fairly quietly but with a sweet singing tone. This will then allow for a contrast in tone for the second phrase (at the upbeat into bar 5). The accompanying Alberti bass should be kept well in the background. A common mistake is to play both hands with the same volume, especially when making a crescendo or in a loud passage. For music of this period, dynamics must not be too extreme, and the notes and chords marked with a *fz* accent should always be contained within the dynamic level of the phrase.

The footnote advises that ornaments are optional, so candidates will not be penalized for leaving them out. However, the turns in bars 5 and 13 should not prove difficult. They flow easily between the beats forming part of the melody. The group of triplet semiquavers (shown above bar 5) is played with the fourth quaver of the left hand.

As the piece should sound like two beats in a bar, a metronome speed of minim = 50–56 will allow it to flow gracefully.

A:4 J. Clarke *A Trumpet Minuet*

A confident, bright attack is needed for this military-style dance. In view of the repeated notes in the opening section and the main melody (at bar 9), it will be effective to play all crotchets (except slurred ones) with a detached touch. Quavers could also be treated in the same way, thus allowing the slurred ones to make a more distinctive impression.

From bar 8 the left hand slips into an accompanying role; extra care will be needed to manage the two parts as they overlap each other. In bar 9 (and similar) many young players will find it impossible to hold the bass minim as they move towards the third beat, in which case it is better to release the first note and produce a neatly shaped slur above. Wherever the completion of the cadence figure occurs (see bar 8), your student should hold the thumb note and lightly detach the crotchets below to form a musically tapered ending.

There are few dynamic marks given, so it would be good to add some more contrast. At bar 12, for instance, a diminuendo would lead to *piano* for the repeat of the previous four bars. The *forte* (bar 17) could be followed by the same treatment for bars 20–4, and again at bar 32. Finally a crescendo in bar 36 would lead to a bold attack for the ending.

A:5 L. Mozart *Allegro in D*

Leopold Mozart devoted much of his life to nurturing the talent of his two children, Nannerl and Wolfgang. Although his keyboard compositions were never highly regarded, they were often written for his children to play, and as such make excellent teaching material.

This cheerful piece in simple ABA form is largely built on ascending scale figures. This is clearly seen in the left hand where the scale starts on the tonic. In the right hand, though, it begins on F♯ (second beat) and these ascending notes should be marked a little so that they stand out from the surrounding notes. There is a liberal amount of fingering given, but, for consistency, the fourth finger may be preferred for C♯ at the start of the penultimate bar of the piece. The shift over the bar-line between bars 2 and 3 (and similar) is a little awkward, and should be practised carefully.

Dynamic marks are also suggested, but if bar 5 begins *piano*, it would be more effective to make a crescendo from the next bar and build to *forte* in bar 8. The middle section begins brightly, but a diminuendo from bar 11, rather than arriving at a sudden *piano* in bar 13, might be preferred. The characteristic left-hand figures in bars 8 and 24 should always be tapered. In the exam room, candidates often give the final note a triumphant bang!

A:6 Mozart *The Bird-catcher's Song*

A search online will offer several staged examples of this aria from *The Magic Flute*, which will help provide inspiration for your student. In them the zany character of Papageno can be seen in his feathery costume, while singing and playing the pipes as he tries to lure a bird into his trap.

In the opera the aria is usually sung at a lively tempo, but in this attractive arrangement, marked *Andante*, a metronome mark of crotchet = 72–80 should be manageable while allowing the cheeky character to come to life.

As this is a modern transcription, it would be best to observe the articulation and dynamics that have been provided. Thus the repeated notes that are not marked staccato (see bar 1) should not be too detached in order that they sound different from staccato quavers; upbeat pairs of semiquavers should be neatly slurred as shown. There may be a tendency for players to hold accompanying quaver notes too long, so careful listening is needed. The *rit.* and pause should be very positive, and a tiny breath taken before resuming pace at the *a tempo*.

It would be a pity not to repeat the flute's flourishes an octave higher (they are marked 'optional'), as the effect adds to the fun of the piece.

B:1 J. Ferrer *Sérénade espagnole (Spanish Serenade)*

This piece may be your student's first introduction to the wonderful world of Spain-inspired music. The solo guitar readily springs to mind here, but equally one can imagine a young man singing to his sweetheart while accompanying himself on the guitar.

The piece consists of two contrasting eight-bar elements, the first melodic and song-like while the second suggests guitar figuration. The exact repetition later on of bars 1–12 means that that there are only 20 bars of music to learn.

An unhurried tempo is suggested by the *Comodo* indication, yet there is always a one-in-a-bar impetus. The opening staccato bars seem to lead naturally towards the appoggiaturas. Well-tapered slurs, with grace notes incorporated unobtrusively, will highlight the sense of longing. A stable bass line is provided by the sustained left-hand dotted crotchets, over which the chords, both equally staccato and very light, add a lilt to the song.

The gentle coaxing mood is somewhat interrupted by the *mezzo-forte* at bar 9. Guitar-like incisiveness will bring the jagged rhythms to life, while the left-hand figures are reliant on nimble fingers. The imperfect cadence midway provides a moment of rest before the tempo resumes.

The last four bars are probably the trickiest in the piece. Firm accents and the rhythmic definition of a flamenco guitarist will give maximum impact as the music reaches its final cadence.

B:2 Vitalij Neugasimov *Lullaby*

The gently soaring right-hand melody and two-in-a-bar rhythmic lilt of this irresistible cradle song is guaranteed to rock even the most restless baby to sleep!

The almost constant quaver movement in the left hand needs careful practice to ensure even tone, with smooth transitions between phrases. Learning the patterns as three-note chords, ideally using a mixture of fourth and fifth fingers (as suggested) on the lowest notes, will help to fix the shapes into the memory.

Good balance between the hands is a key ingredient for a sensitive performance. As always, careful listening will be the best judge. However, in addition, the physical feel of each hand using a different amount of weight can be discovered by shadowing the left hand while playing the melodic line.

Singing the right-hand line at a convenient pitch, breathing at ends of phrases, provides the best clue to discovering the music's natural shape. Although the climax occurs as the highest note is reached in bar 13, the *mezzo-forte* dynamic ensures that the gentle, song-like mood is not disturbed.

The return to the opening music at bar 17 heralds the descent finally into slumber. The last three chords might provide the cue for introducing legato pedalling to your student. Care will be needed to sound all notes when playing very quietly and there should be no hint of shortening the dotted-minim lengths.

B:3 Schumann *Gukkuk im Versteck (Hide-and-Seek)*

Here we get a glimpse of Schumann the family man describing a game probably played by his many children. The start-stop character of the piece depicts vividly, yet subtly, the secretive movements of the players as they creep around trying not to get caught.

Control of tone at *pianissimo* level, especially on an unfamiliar piano, and ensuring that all notes speak, is probably the main challenge here. Rhythms need clear definition, with accurate gauging of rests, which provide time for the hands to move position.

The rising figure with its mixture of slurred and detached notes, suggestive of tip-toe running to a hiding place, occurs four times in the opening section. A feeling of suspense is created by the rests, after which the player perhaps checks warily to right and left at the alternating imperfect and perfect cadences.

The chase that begins in bar 16 only to disperse atumble five bars later is the most demanding section of the piece. Crisp right-hand phrasing, using a light finger action for the staccato notes, contrasts with the more sustained left hand. The crotchets form their own melodic line if held down, and slow practice will ensure that the hands remain safely together. The pause in bar 22 allows the children to catch their breath before the game resumes for one final round of fun.

B:4 Fly *Hot Rolls*

The title of this piece conjures up a scene of large rolls of hay drying in the summer sunshine. It has an unhurried feel which belongs to a bygone age when, according to our perception of it, time seemed to move along more slowly.

The quaver figures generally fit comfortably into rolling five-finger shapes, but the occasional scale figure needs a flexible thumb in order to move smoothly and evenly. Strategically placed rests usually provide ample time for moving to the next hand-position. Projecting the composer's detailed phrasing instructions is the key to providing musical interest. Sufficiently crisp staccatos will contrast with the smoother lines, and moments of imitation between the hands (e.g. bars 5–6) should not be missed. If pedalling is used (this is optional), careful listening will enable the exact moment of depression that avoids catching sounds from the preceding bar (which might occur with the Gs in the penultimate bar, for example).

The contours of the note-patterns, together with the corresponding dynamic shape, seem to convey a gentle undulating countryside. A sufficiently quiet *piano* at bars 9 and 16 will allow maximum impact for the two *forte* climaxes, the second of which is the stronger and more protracted of the two. Added colour is provided by a few unexpected harmonies, and a really quiet, delicate ending will add further subtletly.

B:5 Lysenko *Raindrops*

The delicacy and charm of this character sketch, with its folk-like melodies and alternation between major and minor, make it a delight to play. Any raindrops fall as a light, refreshing shower, perhaps with a brief downpour to finish.

The simplicity of the opening four-bar figure, with its lightly articulated staccatos and offbeat accompaniment, establishes the mood for much of the piece. Attentive listening will ensure that the left hand, which generally plays an accompanying role, balances effectively with its more dominant partner. The subtle variations in texture that occur at each subsequent four-bar phrase add musical interest throughout. The hairpins convey the broad sweep to each phrase at the switch to a minor tonality at bar 5. Co-ordination needs care here, especially when negotiating the contrasting articulation in bar 7, and the minims in bars 9–10 provide a brief harmonic solidity to the otherwise largely syncopated left hand.

Roles are reversed at the return to major in bar 13. Careful control of the right-hand chords will ensure that the new-found assertiveness of the left-hand tune is not spoilt. The final four bars contain some tricky changes of hand-position, which may need isolated practice. The *rit.* and pause seem to suspend time, after which a breath provides the opportunity for repositioning the hands for a confident *forte* finish.

B:6 Nicolai Podgornov *The Little Flower*

The sweet simplicity of this piece seems to capture the beauty, innocence and fragility of a small flower in a garden that is dominated perhaps by larger blooms. It is excellent for developing tone control and will suit a sensitive student.

Flexibly paced quavers, perfectly smooth and even in tone, with a gentle lift at the end of each phrase to allow the music to breathe, will convey the ebb and flow of the melodic line. Choice of tempo is crucial here, in order to give a sense of movement, yet without any haste.

The left hand provides a harmonic cushion throughout, which supports the melodic line discreetly. Although it is impossible to create a completely smooth accompaniment due to repeated notes and some consecutive use of the thumb, isolated practice will help to develop the necessary co-ordination for joining notes where possible – such as in the upper left-hand notes in bars 1–4. Elsewhere, fingering may need to be modified for smaller hands to achieve a seamless transition between chords.

Although the general dynamic level remains *mezzo-piano* throughout, the hairpins encourage a gentle rise and fall to the tone. The changes of key from bar 4 onwards seem to indicate a little more urgency in tempo and mood before the *rit.* leads back to the serene mood of the opening.

C:1 Johnny Mercer *I'm an Old Cowhand*

This wonderfully tongue-in-cheek arrangement portrays a slightly doddery but still charismatic 'Old Cowhand'. To convey the imagery and mood, the piece needs more than accuracy and fluency: musicianship is important, particularly in the first 11 bars where small nuances and dynamic shape should enhance the melody. The middle section is trickier technically with plenty of notated musical detail; performances can readily falter after an easier start, so bar 12 or 13 would be a good place to begin work. Consistent, organized fingering of the chords will help, as will preparing the hand shapes in advance and a confident *forte* tone.

The crucial swung quavers express the cowboy's quirky walk; the mock-skipping staccato dots on the opening riff's crotchets and the first notes of the swung quavers also need characterization. One might, for instance, take a fraction of time on the first bar's fourth beat, slurring it to the next bar's first beat, and/or bring in the second quaver of the swung groupings a touch later than expected (though still in time).

A slightly more relaxed tempo than the one suggested will also work, as long as the playful personality is maintained in the articulation and the right-hand melody is projected with a brighter sound than the accompanying left hand. The minim rest in bar 26 should be taken literally, both to find the final note confidently and to enhance the 'kick of the leg' finish.

C:2 B. Hummel *Prelude*

The improvised world of a prelude provides a wonderful opportunity for the imagination to impose its own story. Here the interest is in warm, pedalled, broken chords, contrasts of articulation, unexpected shifts of harmonies and an attractive initial idea that refuses to go away.

The opening needs to be bewitching with a relaxed approach, each phrase gently shaped within the dynamic with the pedal holding all the notes until the next bar begins. In bar 3 the first semiquaver G should be held underneath the D with the finger, giving time for a smooth, noiseless pedal change that will still catch the lower notes.

The staccato in bars 5 and 7 should be vividly contrasted with short, laughing articulation from the key surface but still shaped towards the following bar, the ascending sequence more demanding in its *forte*. A cheeky little canon in bar 9 fades to a long pause before the opening idea returns. It becomes more and more insistent, ascending in sequence and volume until a grumpy unison – which needs tonal authority and a long pause – attempts to drive it away.

The opening idea sticks in the mind, however, if becoming fainter and slower. Eventually it is as if the performer has had enough. There is a sudden final tantrum, the notes rhythmic, pointed and almost angry – no ritardando at all, just a musical 'slam of the piano lid' to show frustration.

C:3 Kaneda *Gachou no Koushin* (*March of the Geese*)

The translation 'March of the Geese' tells you all that's needed about the character of this comic piece. It relies on a firm sense of the march pulse, the left-hand opening conveying the large webbed feet of the birds while contrasts of articulation and phrasing portray the awkward waddle. The unsubtle crescendo in the quaver repeated chords imitates the geese's ridiculous, unmusical 'honking'.

Your student should start with bars 18 to 25, perhaps learning these from memory, as they present the greatest technical challenge. The coordination is tricky and projecting the left-hand melody will need some conditioning into the hands. Duet practice will pay dividends and simply playing the first right-hand chord of each bar will help the ear expect a projection of the lower part. The numerous repeated notes always need direction in their dynamic and articulation, and the finger changes help the note repeat more reliably.

Dynamic markings need to be properly conveyed. From bar 5, for instance, creating a fabulously descriptive image needs a clearly audible crescendo, the dynamic sustained through bars 6 and 7 then dropping in bar 8, only to start all over again a tone lower.

The editorial tempo gives time for the notated page to be followed, especially the jump to the dal segno and then the coda. If the geese are to have a little more 'Disneyesque' humour, a slightly faster tempo works well too.

C:4 Carol Barratt *Lazy River*

The pentatonic melody here is reminiscent of a Chinese world of pea-pod boats and brightly coloured parasols. It floats on a slow-moving river of luscious chords and atmospheric pedal. The chords' gentle, warm tone is achieved by a relaxed, pliant wrist and some arm weight; the pedal changes must be noiseless, slow and always after the sound. From bar 9 the pedal and left-hand co-ordination becomes a little more crucial; if the finger holds down the first- and fourth-beat left-hand quavers underneath the crotchets, bass notes are held and pedal changes will not be panicked.

The beautiful, evocative melody must be shaped. The articulation in bar 3 reflects only gentle upbeats, and while dynamics change the colour for the whole phrase the melody still needs a delicate rise and fall over each two-bar phrase.

Balance between the hands is challenging. Very light left-hand chords are needed against the right hand's single note, the tune clearly heard but not over-projected. Time should be spent considering the approach to the keys, the touch and the desired sound on just the first quaver beat, building on this until there is tonal control between the hands throughout.

The 'very slow' tempo nevertheless needs a two-in-a-bar lilt. Bar 3 can be a guide, as elegance here is only achievable at an appropriate speed. There might be a slight ritardando at the end with the atmosphere prevailing through the final bar and beyond.

C:5 Garścia *Twisters*

The title is slightly ambiguous, but the essence is of something twisting or spinning, reflected in the initial alternating left-hand figures and even more so in the right-hand semiquavers later on.

Technical ease and control are needed to maintain a seamless, turning ostinato in the first ten bars. In achieving a true legato between the left-hand chords the pianist will learn a wonderful technique for future repertoire. The secret is not to release the previous notes until after the next have sounded, meaning that at some point, if briefly, four notes are heard. The quantity of overlap is part of the musical decision-making.

The haunting yet rhythmically unpredictable melody over the accompaniment needs eloquent shape and a tapered end. The repeat, a delicate echo, is interrupted by the staccato 3rds, and a more energetic and dramatic alternating figure which should drive forwards with all the shape a crescendo can offer; the drama is caught by the abrupt left-hand motif which then gets shorter and softer in its repetition, as if running out of steam.

The *rit.* in bar 17 should be broad enough to allow the right hand to reach the G without panic, and bold enough to calm the gyration before the minim and the return of the opening. This time the left-hand chords stutter, the pulse slows and the twisting circular motion stops, exhausted of energy.

C:6 Heather Hammond *On the Ball*

Listening to James Brown, Herbie Hancock or Funkadelic will help to appreciate the style of this piece. One useful tip to learn and control the left-hand two-bar riff is to memorize it and then use it as the basis for improvisation.

A rhythmic tautness and definition is needed to define the left-hand identity, the tenuto crotchets slightly detached yet precise and the syncopated 3rds across bar-lines held for their full duration. The performance will rely on an authoritative sense of pulse and a straight-eight groove.

The notes have limited interest, putting the onus on the musical shape, dynamic contrast and jazz/rock style 'pushes' (occurring on the weaker beats, for instance on the first F in bar 6). The contrast of the minor middle section also becomes more significant. The change to a softer dynamic needs to be vivid, and the left hand's disrupted ostinato reveals a different feel behind the notes, slightly more lyrical and less emphatic.

A bold and quick crescendo in bar 18 should be followed by driving straight-eight quavers in bar 19, as if waking the band from its reverie, before the 'return'.

Bar 27 begins what is effectively an eight-bar diminuendo, or perhaps an 'outro'. The interest is all in the dynamic control here, with a small *rit.* and pause at the end as the band retire exhausted.

GRADE 3

Perhaps it is time to be a little more adventurous in the choice of pieces, now that exams are more of a familiar experience. Something of quite a different style might broaden the student's outlook, so it is well worth exploring a wide range of repertoire.

A:1 Clementi *Allegro*

This irresistible sonatina movement continues to give pleasure to generations of pianists. Its C major key makes reading the notes fairly effortless; the challenges are in communicating the joyful personality and character.

The right tempo is essential; a lively two-in-a-bar feel is needed, a light third- and fourth-crotchet beat proving counter-intuitive at times as initially they fall under the thumb. All scalic runs should avoid any emphasis on the second minim beat. Articulation will play an important role – detached notes are not uniform but graded according to the context.

As examples, the second right-hand crotchet G in bar 1 should be shorter and lighter than the first; left-hand crotchets are initially played full length but are shorter for bar 3, suggesting movement towards the first beat of bar 4. The left-hand crotchets in bars 6 and 7 should be shorter and lighter as they progress to keep the musical momentum towards a longer *forte* G. The editorial slurs do not imply a break between beats 2 and 3 but are markings more akin to bowing.

The right-hand quavers of bars 7, 13 and 37 are both melody and accompaniment. Some subtlety of control is needed to achieve lighter offbeat quavers and show the melodic line.

The short development section in the tonic minor is delightful and needs a change of tonal colour, followed by a dramatic contrast for bars 20–4 where the melodic line is in the left-hand top crotchets; here a heavy, intrusive right hand should be avoided.

If your student brings to this piece a quicksilver musical mind and good tonal control, imbuing each phrase with charm and humour, the performance will engage audiences and examiners alike.

A:2 J. Clarke *The Bonny Gray Ey'd Morn*

This joyful 'get out of bed' piece will clearly appeal to students of Scottish descent but it is also an excellent opportunity to spark an interest in the different contexts of notation. Some explanation of *notes inégales,* contrasting their French long–short interpretation with the way English Elizabethan composers used a couplet slur to signify the opposite, here a Scotch snap, will help a student's independent learning.

The reversed dotted rhythm here will be counter-intuitive to many students, however, and will need some conditioning into the fingers; there is an obvious added value to practising scales in this rhythm. It is a 'snap' so the semiquaver is almost shorter than notated and slightly emphasized as it is on the beat. Doing this well will also help jazz 'pushes' – a not dis-similar technique.

The two-in-a-bar time signature suggests a buoyant dance character leaving no room for hesitation, so the notes need to be thoroughly under the fingers. Lots of left-hand practice will be particularly required. It will be important to stick religiously to the fingering and make sure all notes are held in bars 1–3 etc. and particularly in bar 7 where the short quavers under the held crotchets are essential to the character.

Light upbeats will help the charm and the right-hand melody should always be clearly prominent above a lighter left-hand accompaniment, except perhaps at the more imitative moments (such as in bars 5 and 6).

Clear dynamic shaping to the first two lines is needed, growing to the middle of the line. The editorial dynamic markings in the second half are excellent, giving a cheeky and playful personality to this theatrical dance.

A:3 D. Scarlatti *Minuet*

This bittersweet dance in the poignant key of C minor seems tinged with sadness. It doesn't always lie under the hand but a little educating into the fingers will soon result in a natural fluency.

One exciting aspect of studying this beguiling piece is the opportunity it presents for making personal musical decisions. Editorial markings suggest one interpretation but examiners will be delighted to hear some-thing refreshing and individual, within a Baroque context. Bars 1–3 and 5–6 could, for instance, be legato throughout with a lift at the bar-line; the quavers of bars 1–3 could alternatively be detached or even phrased to the second beat with the final crotchets lightly detached.

Dynamically, there could be an echo effect between bars 1 and 2, and between bars 5 and 6. Musical ownership of the interpretation can lead to a more convincing performance. Two pervading features are the opening motif's expressive second beat, which needs musical shading, and the contrasting lighter couplets in bars 4, 17 and 19, which give added momentum and dance-like character.

The left hand's held notes are crucial in giving harmonic support to the melodic line, and the minims in bars 10, 11, 14 etc. must sound above the crotchets. This is even more important in bars 21–3 where the left hand goes into two independent parts.

The tempo should allow control and time for the jumps after the double bar, but also capture the charm of the dance. Under the fingers of a musical pianist there is scope for a slightly slower, more relaxed feel to the suggested metronome mark.

Your student might linger a fraction on the final, delicious B♮ in the last bar, a chance to wipe away a tear.

A:4 C. P. E. Bach *Allegro in C*

The personality behind C. P. E. Bach is strongly evident in this piece; it has an almost orchestral feel, with the vivid contrasts in the unison phrases and an engaging rhythmic identity.

Technically there are unpredictable moments so judicious choices of fingering need to be made. Once the physical patterns are in place, the focus can be on the musical decision-making.

A firm two in a bar and decisive articulation of the quavers will both help the drama and convey what is essentially a dance. The left-hand quavers of the first bar should be detached but with a firm, slightly longer bottom C; the following three quavers almost upbeats to the B of bar 2. This bassoon-like articulation might then be continued in the right-hand quavers of bar 2 and matched at the beginning of bar 3.

Thinking in four-bar phrases will help avoid heavy-footedness, particularly in bars 5–8 where a gradual crescendo through the ascending sequence will give musical direction. Conversely, bars 8–12 rely on sudden contrasts between the solo melody and the wonderful, pompous octaves.

Bach plays with the listener's expectations in bars 16 and 17. An anticipated continuation of the scale in bar 16 down to a B and perhaps on to a perfect cadence in G is interrupted by a repetition of the same bar, with the left hand an octave higher, amusing and delighting contemporary audiences. The *piano* marked in bar 17 enhances the joke.

Grace notes should be light and all semiquavers dynamically shaped and under control. To add a little more individuality, a hint of time might be taken before the octaves return in bar 22, as if toying with the listener with a musical wink.

A:5 Haydn *Allegretto in E flat*

Subtitled 'after the second part of the overture' and perhaps intended as an interlude or dance in Haydn's operatic drama *La vera costanza*, this delightful piece has a context that tells us a lot about concerts and audiences of the day; a synopsis of the plot makes entertaining reading.

The piece suits a musical pianist with good technical facility and subtlety of touch. Fifteen bars of continuous right-hand semiquavers (bars 13–27), while engaging in their shape and inventiveness, will need control and above all an imaginative musical personality to convey them with accuracy, charm and musical interest.

Starting with bars 13–27 is advisable. Perhaps learning them from memory, giving them an operatic storyline, and then deciding on the dynamics will help retain accuracy and melodic interest. You might consider a crescendo through bars 17–18 and diminuendo in bars 19–20, for instance, and a crescendo through bars 21–5 with a *subito piano* in bar 26 as if the chorus is poking fun at the soprano's aria.

Bars 28–32 present different challenges: the left hand goes over the right with a coquettish cheek. However, the humour will only work with characterful articulation, technical security and polish, and keeping the repeated B♭s light and unimposing.

Elsewhere, detailed phrasing and a light upbeat will enhance the elegance – as will considering the balance between the hands. The left-hand chords need a relaxed approach; they should never be too loud or coarse in their tone, and in bars 21–6 a legato top to the 3rds will reap huge musical rewards.

The tempo should be graceful. Ensure that it provides space to the rests; a little rhythmic pliancy and nuance between some sections will help give the performance a subtle smile.

A:6 Reinecke *Vivace*

The minor key casts a black cloud over what otherwise seems like a rather jaunty, cheerful song. In fact, all is well, and the glorious change to the major in bar 19 is like a ray of sunshine before the graceful dance of the *con grazia* and the joyful final bar that leaves the audience with a smile.

It is the rhythmic vitality, subtlety of articulation and lightness of touch that gives the piece its character. A light anacrusis, gentle second beats and clearly defined rests will all avoid a heavy-footed approach; the accents are an indication to point the notes but not over-emphasize.

The repeated notes must not be musically static. They need not just a dynamic shape (perhaps a crescendo through the bar), but also a shading of the staccato, keeping it not too short at first to help the musical direction. Effective balance between the hands is also important, and a lighter left hand is crucial in allowing the melody to project without effort.

Bars 15–18 herald the change of mood; in this context tenuto crotchets should be held for their full length, no more than that, and each tenuto is slightly less than the previous to enhance the diminuendo. Staccato quavers should be light and un-snatched with perhaps a hint of a ritardando before the major reprise. This time the melody is *piano*, an important difference to the opening, light-hearted and song-like.

In bars 26–30 a more lyrical and pliant sense of the pulse conveys a graceful dance; the first quaver beat can linger just a fraction. The opening motif fades to the softest *pianissimo* exposing the crotchet rest before the surprise *forte*, which is like a jump for joy.

B:1 Carroll *A Stormy Coast*

The piano music of Walter Carroll has given enjoyment to countless pianists of all ages. Impeccably written for the instrument, the pieces are colourful and always stimulate the imagination; in this case, an exciting description of a storm in the southern seas.

Confident pedalling and free lateral movement across the keyboard will be required. This will provide an excellent opportunity for your student to develop relaxed, flowing arm movements. Most of the pedalling is given in the score, but it would be best to hold the pedal through the first bar (and similar) in order to express the fierce power of the wind and the crashing waves. The rests between the chords do not imply silence here, but are a rhythmic feature; if reassurance is needed, a glance at the last three bars will suffice. In fact the pedalling is not difficult; much of it involves pressing down *with* the chord and releasing *before* the next attack is needed. This type of pedalling adds a slightly percussive edge to the tone and will intensify the dramatic effect.

Dynamics will be very important and should be carefully observed. The weather is squally, the wind blowing fiercely one moment only to fade a few bars later, and an ominous eddy is heard in bars 8–9. Most of the staccato notes are marked with slurs and should be only slightly detached. The given metronome mark is quite sedate (a quicker tempo would make it more stormy), but allow the pace to slacken a little for the last section. Here the storm is passing, and it would be effective to employ the *una corda* pedal for the last three bars.

B:2 Rebikov *Pastushok na svireli igraet* (*The Shepherd Plays on his Pipe*)

A lonely shepherd boy playing to soothe his restless sheep is a familiar Romantic picture. *The Little Shepherd* by Debussy is well-known, and Rebikov's piece bears some resemblance: it has the same key signature, is in the Dorian mode and it contrasts a plaintive melody with a livelier dance-tune. However, this one is in folksong style with a distinctly Russian flavour.

The left-hand part needs to be as smooth as possible, creating a quiet background to the melody above. Simple pedalling would help to join the first chord to the second in each bar, except for bars 3–4 and 18–19 where two-note slurs are a feature of the melody. The chords in the quicker section may prove challenging, especially for players with smaller hands. Like all passages with groups of chords, the secret is to concentrate on those fingers that play the inside notes. Here it will be finger 4 on D in the first chord and finger 3 on E in the next. Practising pairs of notes beginning with the middle ones (where finger 2 has to move from F♯ to G♯ will help to build up familiarity with the shifts.

The 'classical' fingering for grace notes such as those in bars 9 and 11 is 2-4-3; once mastered, it keeps the hand relaxed and gives greater clarity. The tied notes in the final cadence may prove confusing at first. However, if the second finger is deliberately raised just before playing the final chord, it should not be difficult to place the F♯ and lower B while holding the tied notes – unless the hand is not big enough. Then the only solution is to release the top note as the last chord is completed.

B:3 Trad. Spanish, arr. Barratt *Ya se murió el burro* (*The Donkey has Died*)

The character of this children's song is mock-serious rather than sad. The donkey has served the villagers well, and is described as wearing gaiters, jacket, glasses and a red ribbon on its ears before it 'kicked the bucket'!

Starting at bar 3, the phrase structure follows the familiar 2 + 2 + 4 bars, until the dirge-like refrain, which starts at the last quaver of bar 18. Here it should move in four-bar phrases, with the last three bars bringing the piece to a peaceful and valedictory conclusion. A slight crescendo towards the middle of each phrase followed by a diminuendo will give the phrasing expression and an arch-like shape.

This piece can work well with or without pedal. If used it will enhance the tone and help create a smooth sound. Legato pedalling would work best, with a tiny breath or lift of the pedal at the end of bars 4, 6 and 10 to show the phrase-endings. Pedalling can continue when the melody moves to the left hand, but the accompanying chords must always remain at a relatively quieter level as the volume increases.

Because so many of the black keys are played with thumb or fifth finger, it is important to position the hand forward into the keyboard. In the first two bars, for instance, it would be helpful to play all the notes as block chords first (i.e. bar 1 is F♯, B and D) and with the given fingering to see just where the hand lies. There should be as little movement as possible.

Although marked 'very slowly', the music must not drag, and the suggested metronome speed will allow it to flow.

B:4 Gedike *Schulstunde (School Lesson)*

Imagine a classroom on a warm afternoon. It is nearly home-time and the students can't wait to get outside! The teacher talks on, almost without taking a breath, imparting words of wisdom on deaf ears.

The piece has an almost incessant flow of quavers with a few semiquavers to add impetus to the rhythm; there is only one moment (bars 15–16) when the schoolteacher pauses to draw breath. Here a tiny ritenuto would be effective before the teacher sets off again in bar 17.

Slurs and staccato notes must be meticulously observed, together with the given dynamics and nuances. The right hand is kept busy all the time and would benefit from individual attention until it can 'chatter' fluently.

However, the left hand also has passages that will need careful preparation. In bars 9–16 the two-part writing requires reliable fingering so that notes are correctly sustained. For the lower voice in bars 9 and 10, try finger 3 on F and finger 4 on E, with the thumb playing G above. Now the slurred chords in bar 11 can be played more smoothly with fingers 2/4 going to 1/5. In bar 8 the left-hand G would be better played by the thumb.

Pupils often need reminding not to overlook rests. While concentrating on the melody, it would be easy to forget to release some of the left-hand chords on time.

A metronome mark of crotchet = c.84 would be quick enough as long as dynamics are colourful and the articulation lively, and there is no need for a rallentando at the end. One can just hear the teacher ending the day's lecture with the words 'just so'!

B:5 Kullak *Witches' Dance*

Witches conjure up a picture of sinister figures, all in black, riding on their broomsticks. Kullak's brilliantly descriptive dance exudes energy and excitement.

Nimble fingers will be needed for the semiquavers and really crisp staccato for the quavers. If preferred, the rising semiquavers could be played with the fingering 2-1-2-3-4-5 followed by 4 on the first quaver of the next bar. This avoids the thumb passing under in the middle of the group and creates less movement in the hand.

The quiet start is important with only a little increase of tone in bar 7 before dropping back again for bar 9. The sudden *forte* at bar 17 should startle the listener. The dramatic diminished 7th chord appears four times in this passage, perhaps representing the shrieks of the witches as they fly overhead. In bars 17, 21 and 25 pedal could be used to add tone and colour. It could also be used in bars 50 and 52, only here the overall dynamic level is *piano* so the *sfz* accents should not be too strong.

After reaching *fortissimo* at the climax in bar 28, the music suddenly drops to *piano* again; it would be helpful to memorize the next four bars so that eyes can be on the keyboard as the music leaps downwards from octave to octave. With the start of the reprise at bar 33 the *una corda* pedal will help to create an eerie atmosphere for the eight bars of *pianissimo*; it could be used again for the last three bars as the witches disappear into the mist. A metronome mark of dotted crotchet = c.72 will catch the hurly-burly of this exhilarating dance.

B:6 H. Reinhold *Ariette*

The romantic mood of this poignantly nostalgic miniature will appeal to the more sensitive of your students. It requires a beautiful singing tone and carefully balanced voicing, but is otherwise technically undemanding.

Marked to be played *In mässiger Bewegung* (in moderate tempo), it needs to flow comfortably, one in a bar, at dotted crotchet = *c*.48. It is like a duet with the melody passing from hand to hand. The dotted-note figures should never sound jerky, but glide along smoothly and gently. Pedal can be used when the right hand has the melody, changing on the first beat of each bar, but it is not essential. Only in bar 8 (and similar) will it be necessary to make an extra change for the third beat. Pedalling the left-hand melody would be more complicated and best avoided at this early grade.

Whether using the sustaining pedal or not, the accompanying chords must be as legato as possible so that the mood is not disturbed. The fingers should be kept in contact with the keys and a light arm used to weigh the chords down, especially if not employing the pedal. The given fingering works well and there are no awkward stretches to be negotiated. If observed, the dynamic marks will provide a clear outline for the performance, although the player must feel the rise and fall of the melody to give expression to the phrasing. A slight ritenuto is all that is needed to shape the last two bars.

If you are looking for an alternative for List B, this lovely piece will fit the bill and give pleasure to player and listener alike.

C:1 Franklyn Gellnick *Moody Prawn Blues*

Whether or not the intriguing title of this piece appeals to your pupil, its laid-back 'moody' character cannot fail to ensure it is a popular exam choice.

An easy-going tempo and gentle swung rhythms which sound natural rather than 'worked out' are the main keys to a stylish, spontaneous performance. Practising a scale, perhaps D minor, with swung quavers is a useful starting point to gaining fluency in these jazzy rhythms.

The opening four-bar introduction, with its measured bass line and smoother quavers which follow, sets the scene. The right-hand 6ths will need practice in order to shift the thumb while sustaining the upper notes. The off-beat accents are characteristic features which end most phrases throughout the piece.

Starting the middle section at bar 9 sufficiently gently allows a sense of growth through the sequence that follows in which a smooth, agile thumb will prevent any awkward bumps in the rising quavers. The main climax at bar 12 is heightened by the 'funky' left-hand chord with its C/D♭ clash – a reliable four-in-a-bar pulse will ensure that it is correctly placed off the beat.

Bar 18 may prove a tricky corner as both hands travel towards the chord; however, moving the left hand in towards the black keys will prepare the thumb for playing the B♭. Rests at this point and two bars later should be given their full length. Slightly detaching the second chord in bars 20 and 22 will allow the hand to move easily to the next position while at the same time giving prominence to the accent which follows. A well-graded diminuendo through to the final pizzicato-like bass note will add a subtle touch to the end.

C:2 Nikki Iles *Cotton Reel*

The atmosphere of a graceful, lilting Deep South dance is conjured up in this delightful piece. Its constant alternation between dotted-crotchet and crotchet beats adds an intriguing rhythmic twist.

Initially subdividing into six quavers per bar will ensure accurate note-lengths, but the transition to feeling the pulse in crotchet and dotted-crotchet beats must be made for a convincing lilt to emerge.

A legato touch works well for much of the right-hand melodic line. Each 3rd should sound exactly together; the occasional staccato detail, played lightly and not too short, adds phrasing interest. Gently detaching the left hand's dotted crotchets can provide definition to the main beats and the rising quaver figures are worthy of slight prominence.

Each long phrase has its natural ebb and flow. Dynamics never rise beyond *mezzo-forte* and hairpins offer subtle shading. A slight increase in intensity is suggested from the ascending phrase at bar 16, yet rhythmic poise must remain. Faithfully observing note-lengths, especially the ties, enriches the texture. Care is also needed to keep the right hand's non-tune notes subdued to avoid confusion with the main melody.

Although most of the piece can be played effectively without pedal, using it in the last bar (as indicated) is necessary for sustaining both notes of the left-hand 10th. Wise candidates will place the foot close to the pedal before starting the performance in order to prevent a scramble as this bar approaches!

C:3 Philip Martin *Jack is Sad*

Sensitive players will be drawn to the haunting folk-like melody and modal harmony of this enchanting piece, which seems to evoke both a charm and melancholy typical of the Irish character.

The spacious tempo allows time for the changes of hand-position to be negotiated easily. Although some judicious touches of pedal will help to sustain the harmonies, there is no substitute for good finger legato. Care is needed in the release of notes at the correct moment while the tied left-hand notes are held for their full length.

A natural rise and fall in dynamic will mirror the arch-like contours of each of the three main phrases. Starting the piece sufficiently quietly gives opportunity for growth within a gentle scale. The main melodic line can be highlighted by keeping the inner accompanying notes subdued in bars 5–7 as the tone decreases; the dotted minim, which ends this phrase, should not be cut short.

The following phrase has a more intricate, somewhat meandering shape. Its climax only reaches *mezzo-forte*, ensuring that the gentle mood is not disturbed; the echo on the repeated phrase adds a haunting quality when played sufficiently quietly. The sharps in bars 17–18 add extra poignancy to the harmony and a slight separation at the right-hand phrase-endings will allow the musical line to breathe. Mordents, played lightly on (not before) the beat, serve to enhance the melodic line.

Bar 18 sees the start of the final phrase, a slight variation of the opening one. The ambiguous final chord, approached by a well-graded diminuendo, ensures that the melancholy mood remains to the ending. The bass A should be placed exactly on the third beat and the sense of calm created by the pause is to be savoured.

C:4 Mike Schoenmehl *Melancholy*

The chromatic shifts and unhurried tempo give this piece a laid-back, contemplative mood, as if lost in thought. The almost identical repetition of the first eight bars at the end means that there are only 12 bars of notes to learn – a bonus for many pupils!

Clear legato lines, with no overlap of sounds, are essential throughout. The pedal, released on each harmonic change, will enrich the outer sections, but equally the lines may be sustained solely by finger legato. Playing the right-hand melodic line without its inner accompanying notes, using the fingering marked (or, better still, singing it), is a good starting point for understanding the texture. In bars 1–2 the left-hand minims provide bass support and quiet thumb notes in both hands will allow the melody to project clearly.

Despite the time signature, the phrases will flow more easily when thinking in two minim beats per bar. The diminuendo in the opening one-bar phrases produces a sigh-like effect, which is in contrast to the arch shape that follows. If playing without pedal, the fingers can sustain the upper line of bars 3–4 while the thumb moves gently and unobtrusively – a co-ordination skill probably needing isolated practice. The syncopated rhythms and crescendo that end the section in bars 7 and 8 give a more abrupt, jagged feel. Here, exam nerves must not cause shortening of the long notes and rests.

The pared-down texture and quieter dynamic midway suggest a more carefree mood. Again, good rhythmic control is important and right-hand rests should be allowed to punctuate the phrasing. The right hand's semibreve must be sustained throughout bar 10.

Finally, a surprising touch is provided by the last note of the piece, played *pianissimo*, exactly on its time-spot and at the correct octave.

C:5 Seiber *Foxtrot II*

Imagining this lively piece played by a 1930s dance band, foot-tappingly rhythmic and fun, will give your student the right picture. Its energetic, jazzy rhythms and catchy tune make it an ideal choice for pupils with strong, reliable fingers and a good sense of pulse.

The trickiest 'corners' in a piece, in this case probably bars 7–8, often serve as indicators of the tempo that is most suitable. Although a two-in-a-bar feel is needed for the dance to take off, the printed metronome mark of minim = *c*.112 may well be over-ambitious for some Grade 3 players.

The left hand plays the important role throughout of maintaining a firm pulse. Initially practising each bar as chords will help to secure the shapes in the finger memory. A detached touch, light and airy, especially on off-beats, will create a buoyant accompaniment that never overpowers the melody. The accent in bar 8, which kick-starts the crotchets after the rests, and the linking descending scale in bar 24 are worthy of highlight, and the D♮ in the final bar should not be mistaken for a B♮.

Slow practice, subdividing into four crotchet beats, will help to co-ordinate the hands. Your student might imagine a saxophone playing the right-hand line, decisive, slightly detached, in order to ensure that all repeated notes sound, and with clear accents to highlight the syncopations.

The absence of dynamics allows your students free rein to explore their own ideas. While a firm, bright tone seems to suit much of the piece, dropping down to *piano* as the tonality switches to A minor in bar 17 provides relief before a build-up towards the return to the home key. Either a loud or quiet ending is possible, according to preference – the composer has left the choice open.

C:6 Jesús Torres *Aurora*

Although some pupils may be put off by the unfamiliar tonality, the imaginative textures and pedal effects of this piece offer a good introduction to a twenty-first-century idiom. The title, meaning 'sunrise', suggests early morning; perhaps a calm, warm summer one. An impressionistic effect is created by the use of pedal throughout, and the gradual creeping-up in pitch evokes the dawning of the sun.

The pedal also plays a key role in sustaining harmonies and adding tonal resonance. A keen ear and accurate co-ordination of hands and foot will ensure that all sounds clear on each harmonic change, in addition to letting the air in at the rests which occur at the beginning of some bars.

Note learning always needs an especially vigilant eye and ear in a piece with no obviously recognizable key-centre. Accidentals carried through the bar can be easily missed and the *8ve* signs need care. Smooth, gentle quavers at the opening set the calm scene, distant and veiled. Keeping the fingers close to the keys will aid control here, and no unwanted bumps should occur at changes of hand-position. The high B♭ in bar 5 suggests the appearance of a single ray of sun through the early morning mist. In bars 7–8 good control will be needed to fit the right-hand syncopations effortlessly around the accompanying thumb quavers, and a well-managed crescendo and diminuendo will create new warmth to the tone.

The sparser texture from bar 10, as the sun begins to rise to its full height, poses its rhythmic challenges. Longer notes should be given full value, and the temptation to hurry at the crescendo resisted, with syncopations accurately placed. Each note must sound in the very quiet, serene chords at the end.

GRADE 4

Many of the List B pieces will now benefit from some pedal, but if you feel that your student is not quite ready, don't forget that further options are available beyond ABRSM's own volumes of selected exam pieces. The musical personality of students often becomes more firmly established at this stage and they can play to their strengths, making the most of contrasts in mood and character within the music.

A:1 Hummel *Tempo di Menuetto*

Minuets regularly appear in the A lists of the ABRSM syllabus, and there is probably no better way to familiarize oneself with the style than to listen to the many examples in Haydn's and Mozart's music. The suggested tempo of crotchet = *c.*120 can be taken as a minimum, and a faster tempo, up to say crotchet = *c.*132, could benefit the sense of style, allowing a more dance-like character.

Although the time signature is 3/4, a one-in-the-bar feeling can be developed to lift the music and to avoid a syllabic effect. A very gentle lean into the downbeats will help, perhaps with slightly more emphasis on the peaks of phrases such as those at bars 3 and 35. Fingerwork should be rhythmic and even; the printed fingering is useful in this regard, although in bar 2 (and later equivalents) using a right-hand finger 2 on the initial C may facilitate negotiation of the 3rds that appear later in the bar.

There is quite a robust, cheerful feeling for much of the piece, so dynamic contrasts need to be strong, especially where *forzando* or *fortissimo* is juxtaposed with *piano*. However, the offbeat *fz* should be played according to its context and therefore stressed rather than hammered out. Use of the pedal is not necessary, although occasional dabs on the first beat of the bar, for example in bars 1–8, can complement any slight downbeat emphases.

This piece may appear to be quite extended but, given that the A section is repeated between bars 33 and 48, there is not so much to learn after all!

A:2 Kirnberger *La lutine (The Mischievous Sprite)*

As befits a musical depiction of a mischievous sprite, this piece is short and lively, and appropriate musical imagery can inform your student's interpretation – but first, the notes!

A crisp staccato touch from a firm fingertip and convex first joint will work well for any unslurred quavers. If the suggested right-hand articulations are followed, it would be a good idea, for the sake of consistency, to duplicate these as appropriate in the left-hand part. Scale practice will benefit the runs, although the trickiest right-hand passage (bars 13–14) can be practised as a series of three-note chords fingered 4/2/1 (e.g. F♯/D/B) followed by a single note (A) played with the fifth finger. This pattern could then be modified to two notes played together (e.g. F♯/D) followed by two played singly, before attempting the passage as notated.

The suggested speed of crotchet = *c*.104 yields a safe tempo, fast enough to convey the piece's mischievous character but steady enough to encourage precision. However, the character will not be lost and may even be enhanced if a slightly faster pace is adopted – as long as control of rhythm and pulse is not compromised. The indicated dynamics are editorial and therefore need not be heeded, but they work well musically. Nevertheless, your student might consider playing *mezzo-piano* from the upbeat into bar 9, dropping to *piano* four bars later before gradually increasing in volume to reach *forte* at the upbeat into bar 17.

A generally light, dance-like approach that avoids extremes of *forte* will effectively convey the image of a sprite that is mischievous rather than evil – and in the exam students will need to remember to play the first repeat!

A:3 Stölzel *Bourrée*

Despite its minor key this music is both lively and sturdy, thereby betraying its dance origins – which should be made apparent in any performance.

As with all bourrées, the time signature indicates a two- rather than a four-in-the-bar feel, so a gentle emphasis on the first crotchet of the bar and an even gentler one on the third will help to convey the metre. This should not be too difficult to achieve given that many of the notes that fall on the second and fourth crotchets (i.e. the half beats) are in the nature of passing notes and don't invite any highlighting from the pianist.

Crotchets can be played detached – a string player might use the word 'portato' rather than staccato – but quavers may be more legato (as the editor suggests), thereby avoiding an overdose of hopping! Dynamic suggestions, also editorial, are musically helpful. However, for more contrast, your student might like to play *piano* from bar 16, second crotchet, to bar 20, third crotchet. Even when playing *forte*, heaviness should be avoided;

in performance, therefore, physical movements can be constrained, with the wrist and forearm springy rather than floppy.

The music's dance-like character will emerge if the tempo is minim = *c*.88 but, for more confident students, a slightly faster tempo will add an extra touch of zest. Whatever tempo is adopted, a steady pulse is crucial, so practising with a metronome would be beneficial. Rubato is not needed at any point except perhaps towards the very end where the final chord may be stylishly arpeggiated.

A successful performance of this engaging piece will get a Grade 4 programme off to a buoyant start.

A:4 J. S. Bach *Invention No. 1 in C*

Bach's two-part inventions are an excellent introduction to simple polyphonic playing and are invaluable for developing co-ordination of the hands. Although preliminary learning stages (to establish, for example, suitable fingerings) will almost certainly involve hands-separate work, practising will generally need to be done hands together. The art of good part-playing lies in the skilful synchronization of opposing finger motions, which practising with one hand cannot, by its very nature, achieve.

One aspect of co-ordination that may need thought is ornamentation. If your edition suggests a four-note mordent in the right hand commencing on the upper note, and your student finds this awkward, the ornament can be reduced to three notes by starting on the fundamental. These notes can be matched to the left-hand semiquavers by playing the first two as demisemiquavers.

A tempo of crotchet = *c*.72 keeps the music moving without any sense of hurry and, while the beat needs to be stable, subtle touches of rubato at cadence points are not inappropriate (e.g. the end of bar 6 going into bar 7, bar 14 going into bar 15, and the final two bars). In terms of shape, the oft-repeated seven-note semiquaver figures should be eased in with no sense of emphasis on the first note and with a feeling of moving towards the third beat. The modulations in the second half of the piece suggest a raised intensity of expression so the dynamic level may likewise be raised. A legato approach to the music works well, although octave leaps in the left hand perhaps invite a more detached touch.

This piece offers an attractively fresh opener to a Grade 4 recital programme.

A:5 Haydn *Allegro in F*

This delightful piece is full of the good humour for which its composer is renowned. One means of conveying its character is by crisp but light staccato quavers, the finger snatching upwards and inwards out of the key while preserving economy of movement. Although staccato scales are not required by the ABRSM syllabus until Grade 7, there is nothing like being ahead of the game, and staccato scale practice could be very helpful as preparatory work.

A tempo of crotchet = *c*.112 will provide adequate momentum for the mood but, for your more nimble students, up to *c*.126 will add extra panache – as long as the pulse is controlled and there is no dragging or rushing. The hardest passage in technical terms is probably the chordal sequence in bars 9–12. If the right hand starts on fingers 5/3/1 and the left hand on 5, then the hand-position stays roughly the same for two bars. Chord-shapes and fingerings are then sequentially repeated a tone lower, from the last quaver of bar 10. Consistency of hand-position may outweigh the disadvantages of using the left-hand thumb on the B♭ in bar 11.

If your student is using the Universal Edition, then the dynamic suggestions should prove helpful. However, to preserve the Classical balance of the music, it might be prudent to imagine them all a little quieter (perhaps, for example, aiming for *forte* rather than *fortissimo* near the end). As always, contrasts will need projection; exaggeration when practising may therefore be a useful strategy although, in performance, proportion should be restored.

Examiners will enjoy performances that capture the sparkle and humour of this piece.

A:6 J. L. Krebs *Klavierstück (Allegro) in E flat*

Krebs may not be a very familiar name but he was a student of J. S. Bach and highly regarded by the great man. Krebs was a man of his time and here he adopts an early Classical manner.

Much of the phrasing is in four-bar units so it is useful to determine the natural contours. In the opening phrase (and similar places) the right-hand semiquavers seem to guide the ear towards the gentle dissonance of the first beat of bar 3, which can be discreetly emphasized. Little by way of articulation is printed so this will need to be considered. Right-hand semi-quavers may be played legato while left-hand quavers will sound well when played detached, if not ostentatiously staccato. However, slurring may sometimes be desirable. For example, the quavers forming the first beat of bar 3 (left hand) can be paired together to create a gentle emphasis which serves to support phrase-shaping in the right. A general dynamic framework of *mezzo-piano* works nicely and nuances can be applied against this background. The thickest texture occurs at bar 21, suggesting the climax of the piece, after which a general diminuendo is effective.

A tempo of crotchet = *c.*80–8 yields a manageably flowing pace wherein the semiquavers will need to be even. Although performing the semiquavers staccato seems inappropriate, practising them in this manner will aid clarity and finger independence. The pulse needs to be stable, and no rubato is needed except perhaps for a slight fermata at the double bar and a small ritenuto towards the end.

This piece makes extensive use of scales and broken chords so it could be instructive for your student to work out which keys these belong to.

B:1 Estévez *Canción para dormir una muñeca (Lullaby for a Doll)*

This jewel of a piece with its blend of tenderness, childhood innocence and melancholy may be a new discovery for many teachers. If so, you and your student are in for a real treat!

The simple folk-like melody, which falls naturally into two-bar phrases, is accompanied by the most subtle harmonic cushion of left-hand chords; it is modal in feel and becomes more chromatic as the piece unfolds. *Legatissimo* left-hand 3rds can be produced by the fingers alone in the opening bars. However, changes of hand-position may need isolated practice in order to produce smooth, unobtrusive joins. Although judicious fingering will go part way towards creating legato chords from bar 9 onwards, the smoothest effect will be created by the pedal. Critical listening will ensure that the pedal is released sufficiently and at exactly the right moment to clear all harmonies. The delicious mix of two harmonies in the penultimate bar can be enjoyed, before the final G major chords.

Singing the melody at a convenient pitch, breathing at phrase-ends, will give a guide as to a suitable, flowing tempo at the start. The indications later on suggest, in effect, a gradual slowing down from bar 13, as the doll is finally lulled into sleep.

Good key control will ensure that dynamic levels never become over-robust, breaking the gentle, sleepy atmosphere. Ornaments, played as lightly as possible either on or before the beat, must not interrupt the rhythmic flow. The change of register at bar 14, hushed to a whisper, is a particularly lovely moment which benefits from use of the *una corda* pedal. The tied B♭s in bars 17 and 19 should be noticed; also the offbeat placement of the *pianissimo* chord in the penultimate bar.

B:2 Rybicki *Hej, znam ja łączkę (I Know of a Pleasant Meadow)*

Clothing a simple folksong in modern harmonies, a technique explored by many twentieth-century composers, creates an interesting link between past and present. Here the melody has a fresh appeal and the constantly changing accompaniment ensures that musical interest is always sustained.

The opening four bars announce, like a fanfare, the main 'song'. Fingering the left-hand chromatic 3rds as printed allows them to be played legato in contrast to the right-hand staccato, and the pause provides breathing space before the *a tempo* at bar 5.

Singing the 16-bar verse at an unhurried *Andantino* tempo, breathing every four bars, is a good starting-point for understanding the phrasing – which the frequent, and usually sudden, changes in dynamics underline. The chromaticisms and gentle tone at the outset seem to suit smooth, expressive lines, whereas the *forte* at bar 13 suggests a more robust, phrased approach. Holding the tied notes in bars 14–21 for their full value will enrich the texture, and care will be needed not to confuse the right hand's inner notes with the main tune.

The canon at bar 21 is an unexpected feature reliant on strong finger-work and matching articulation to highlight the imitation between the hands. The *mezzo-piano* phrases might benefit from some pedal, changed at each bar, to enhance the harmonies; students should also watch out for the accidentals in this section.

The last eight bars serve as a postlude. A sense of winding down is provided by a well-graded diminuendo over the entire eight bars matched by an equally gradual rallentando over the final three. Depressing the pedal momentarily after sounding the A major chord in the penultimate bar will ensure that no unwanted sounds are caught from the previous chord.

B:3 Schumann *Jägerliedchen (Huntsman's Song)*

This bright, bustling character piece vividly evokes a hunting scene, with horn calls and riders on horseback. While the rhythms must convey two, not six beats in a bar, the energy is created more by phrasing and accentuation rather than by speed. Cantering rather than galloping rhythms will give poise to the music while ensuring clarity and accuracy in the detail.

The opening horn call, which acts as a motif throughout, immediately captures the listener's attention. The pedal serves to add extra resonance to the octave texture, and at subsequent appearances it allows the hand to move to a new position in advance of playing. Some preliminary staccato training, perhaps using a scale or five-finger pattern, may be necessary to ensure that both hands have equal clarity and definition. A finger staccato works well for the quieter moments after the double bar, whereas a wrist touch will provide the greater strength needed elsewhere. Initially, however, practising the quaver figures legato will help to establish the notes in the finger memory.

The boisterous character for much of the piece needs firm, bold attack, especially on the accents. Bars 17 to the end, which provide the guide to a sustainable tempo, are likely to prove the most challenging. Momentum must not be allowed to slacken as quavers and left-hand horn motif combine; detached crotchets will ensure rhythmic buoyancy, especially when offbeat quavers are kept light. If the right-hand stretches prove troublesome (e.g. bars 21–2), the lower note of the octaves may be omitted, or reallocated to the other hand. The two *piano* phrases provide welcome contrast, and the accented G in bar 25 is a quirky touch which momentarily seems to disturb the otherwise regular rhythms.

B:4 Bortkiewicz *Russian Peasant Girl*

There is something unmistakably Russian about this piece, which seems to capture perfectly the centuries-old toil and routine of peasant life. The singable melody, repetitive and narrow in range, together with its regular rhythmic patterns, has a folk-like character, and added interest is provided by the snippets of left-hand melody.

Strong fingers, supported by a relaxed, flexible wrist, will enable the uppermost melody to project over the chords. The pedal plays a vital role throughout in sustaining the harmonies, but good fingering will also help to ensure smooth transition between chords. Exam candidates occasionally experience difficulty in adapting to an unfamiliar pedal – and the ear is the best guide to exactly when, and how far, to release it in order to clear each harmony fully. Most bars require only two changes, but those containing chromatic shifts may need more frequent clearing. An additional refinement might be to omit the pedal temporarily for the detached repeated quavers.

The minor tonality at the start immediately establishes the melancholy mood. Imagining the speed of walking, slightly trudging and careworn, will achieve the ideal tempo; it should flow with two (rather than four) beats in a bar. The change to the major midway, together with its louder dynamic and poignant echo four bars later, offers a brief glimmer of optimism before the tonality slips back to minor for the final section. Although much of the piece is marked *piano* or quieter, there is plenty of subtle inflection to be found, particularly where the chromaticisms add greater intensity. The opportunity for highlighting the left hand when it takes centre stage should not be missed, and good control of both tone and pacing will capture the sense of calm, perhaps also desolation, at the ending.

B:5 Czerny *Exercise in B flat*

The title 'Exercise' is not going to inspire students to choose this piece, but change it to 'Romance' or, perhaps, 'Love Song' and it seems much more appealing! It is an excellent piece for developing a cantabile tone and sensitive balance between the hands.

Ranking the three strands of the texture in the first section in order of importance is a good starting-point to understanding the song-like character. The bass notes, which should be sustained for their full length, provide support for the right-hand melody, while subdued repeated thumb notes serve to maintain gentle momentum. Imagining the melody sung or played on an instrument will give the clue to sustaining and shaping each of the opening three phrases. The left hand momentarily assumes a more prominent melodic role in bar 4, and the *sforzando* two bars later should be considered within the context of the overall gentle dynamic level.

The right-hand 3rds after the double bar need careful co-ordination to ensure that both notes sound together. The cello-like bass line helps to create intensity at the approach to the climax point as G minor is briefly stated, followed by an equally shapely retreat back towards the *dolce* four bars later. Although the ornament in bar 15 fits neatly into four demisemiquavers, which coincide with the left-hand A, decorations – as always in this expressive style – need a spontaneity and slight freedom, as if improvised.

Melodic differences enhance the return to B♭ major at bar 17. The suspensions in bar 19 are especially lovely if well-tapered. The semiquavers three bars later, which again call for spaciousness and elasticity, represent a flight of fancy, reminiscent of an opera singer's coloratura, before the piece ends calmly and simply.

B:6 Fuchs *Morgenlied (Morning Song)*

This charming piece, somewhat reminiscent of Schumann's shorter pieces, has the appeal of an early morning walk – fresh and clear before the summer sun has had a chance to warm the air.

Organized right-hand fingering, especially when playing two notes together, ensures that the melodic line is perfectly legato, and a slight punctuating breath where marked adds definition to the phrasing. Initially playing the left hand in crotchet chords will help in understanding the harmonic framework – which often seems to span more bars than is indicated by the printed phrase-marks. Firm bass notes on the main beats, some of which are sustained as crotchets, support the melodic line; keeping the offbeat chords quieter will encourage that all-important two-in-a-bar feel to the rhythm.

The term *Einfach* (also often used by Schumann) provides the clue to the overall mood and implies an easy-going, unhurried tempo which allows space for the melodic lines to meander gently. Subtle rubato will enhance this simple, artless character, and all shaping of undulating song-like melody should be gentle and sensitive. The brief excursions to B minor at bars 7 and 15 suggest moments of greater intensity, as does the ascent to the musical peak at bar 22. The pedal adds richness to the texture at this point and the slower harmonic rhythm gives the effect of time suspended, as if pausing to admire the view from the top of a hill.

A gradual diminuendo through the final five bars, without becoming over-quiet too soon, produces the most satisfying (and controllable) descent. The right-hand appoggiatura in the penultimate bar, if well shaped and with the chord held for its full length, provides a final poetic gesture.

C:1 D. C. Glover *Indian Pony Race*

This is perhaps less the 'pony club' and more the open countryside of Virginia and the training of a wild Chincoteague Pony. Therein lies the solution to practising the piece: it is wild and exciting but requires physical discipline, patience and understanding.

The musical pony, having been caught, needs breaking in: careful fingering should precede a slow education of the notes into the fingers, noting bars that are repeated. Consistency of fingering is crucial, especially in the right-hand chords (bars 3 and 4 etc.) where there must be no hesitation when the harmony changes. Practising these offbeat against the bass notes will help, as will using a 5/3/1 rather than 4/2/1 fingering.

A more robust kick of the hind legs in the bass notes, and lighter chords in the right, will convey leaping and bucking; the shake of the mane in bar 6 needs every little ruffle clearly defined. Experimenting with the semiquavers, drumming on the piano lid, will help consolidate the rhythm: a shake of the wrist on to the fingertips will help develop a quick, relaxed wrist staccato for all the passages involving semiquavers.

The pony calms down and behaves itself from bar 11, but the pianist requires continued concentration and control. A relaxed bounce from the left wrist is essential here, and the crescendo and diminuendo hairpins give just a hint of unease.

The final five bars need good anticipation, the frisky character challenging the performer's hands to jump confidently to new positions. Rhythmic work and shadow jumping will help the control and leave the performer greater freedom to enhance the final crescendo with held pedal – the lively pony leaping the fence and making a bid for freedom!

C:2 Mike Cornick *In the Shed*

Just what is being built in this shed is a mystery – but the occupier is clearly in a cheerful mood, whistling an irritatingly persistent yet catchy motif that first appears in bar 2.

A strong, rhythmic bass line conveys chirpy good humour; it needs a feel behind the syncopation to provide a rhythmic backbone for the swung melodic phrases. This may be used as the basis for some improvisatory work, repeating the four-bar left-hand phrases while improvising melodically on a blues scale on C. Rests, articulation and offbeat pushes play an important part in giving the music vitality and energy – the end of left-hand crotchets clearly defined and quavers before the bar-line given a slight emphasis.

The piece is a theme and two variations, but given the limited melodic contrast there needs to be a wider range of dynamics, and more tonal colour and shape than what is suggested by the rather sparse markings. Fun can be had varying the sound of the repetitive melodic phrase.

The tempo needs careful consideration too: it must neither rush nor be frantic. Character and cheek are possible at the suggested crotchet = 150, but a slightly slower tempo of crotchet = *c*.136 will still give a jaunty feel, providing that the phrasing is clear and the pulse sustained throughout.

The most difficult bars, rhythmically, are bars 7–8 because of the unpredictability in the shape. In bar 17, the inner parts need to be kept gently out of the way. A large crescendo is essential towards the end. Cleanly observing the last quaver rests will emphasize the 'that's it!' nature of the final crotchets as the shed-built creation is revealed with panache.

C:3 Prokofiev *Progulka (Promenade)*

This may be a Russian (or French) promenade but the image is universal. The gentle one-in-a-bar conveys an image of the slow arm-in-arm stroll of our promenading couple, but the three lively crotchets in the bar convey the more purposeful bustle of other people around them.

The melodic line is conversational, so putting words to the notes (with perhaps 'take my hand' for the first phrase) will help give independence to the bass part and encourage dynamic shape and rhythmic nuance – as Prokofiev's tenuto markings indicate. The left hand can have a holiday-like playfulness, keeping the triplets light and avoiding too many heavy first beats. A slight relaxation through the crotchets in bar 4 will allow the tune flexibility.

As the footnote suggests, the middle section from bar 20 implies more of a conversation between the couple; again the upper and lower melodies need a relaxed feel, dynamic shape, and a well co-ordinated legato line. The left hand here could easily spoil the overall mood, so the couplets should not be too short or intrusive. The section ends with a question mark, a delightful four bars in which a three-note phrase ascends. There is the strongest suggestion of a ritardando then a slight pause over the G in bar 36.

The discussion then becomes livelier and moves to the left hand, with some significant jumps. A little time taken here will prevent unwanted accents and show the different voices. The left hand has to convey a some-what flirtatious and reconciliatory exchange both above and below the gentle right-hand accompaniment. The rests should be used to enable a quick jump, preparing the sound of the next note, as the couple begin to disappear into the distance.

C:4 Bartók *Der Stampfer (Topogó; Pe loc)*

Bartók's Romanian Folk Dances are worth exploring both in their original piano version and in Bartók's own orchestration. They are delightfully evocative pieces and the melody of this particular dance, 'In One Spot', is based around an Aeolian scale on B with a wonderful gypsy-like augmented 2nd adding to its poignancy.

The drone-like left hand needs to appear almost out of nowhere. With the hand balanced and fingers close to the keys, the notes can float in like a curl of smoke; this is best achieved by putting the pedal down before the first bar. Over the top of this the melody should sing through like a violin or flute, articulated as marked within the held pedal, and dynamically shaped towards the clear, tambourine-like mordents and accents. Rounded fingers and not too much arm weight will help achieve the desired clarity.

Overall shape to the longer phrases – for example rising dynamically to the longer syncopated note over bars 6–7 then falling away – will help avoid the piece becoming too fragmented. Indeed the whole movement has a natural rise and fall, with a climax in bars 20–7 before the piece retires into the distance phrase by phrase.

Each change of harmony in the left hand necessitates a change of pedal and, despite the impression given by the placement of the brackets, it is crucial to catch all the left-hand chords. The bars of left-hand rests give an immediate transparency to the texture, highlighting the articulation and heralding, firstly, the bright central D major section with its intense left-hand augmented 4ths, but then helping the sound to die away. The left hand descends and the tempo slows as if the dancers fall asleep one by one until there is nothing but silence.

C:5 Brian Chapple *Parade*

This is a cheerful, festive piece with a carnival atmosphere and infectious humour; it is rich in drum-like left-hand figures, bugle and clarinet right-hand chords, gossipy quavers, and staccato phrases.

A good starting-point is to establish a context, perhaps imagining a picture of the parade and then creating sounds to support the visual idea. The effectiveness of the performance will undoubtedly lie in rhythmic precision, articulation and dynamic contrasts. Feeling the rhythmic character by tapping out the rhythm and articulation on a table top or piano lid will give the perfect framework upon which to hang the notes.

Technical work might be needed to achieve the right sounds. Developing a drop and lift of the wrist will enhance the opening couplets; a precise bounce at the wrist for the right-hand 3rds encourages a vibrant, clear staccato with a reliable tone; and an over-holding of the lower notes in the left-hand quavers will create contrast, a musical line, and avoid an intrusive repeated D. The 3rds in particular require a good, confident physical memory, but they can be grouped into hand-positions. Practising them in chords of four notes will help fluency.

A quick mind and hands are needed to make sure there are no hesitations between phrases to unsteady the procession; using the rests to get ready for the next note will help. It is also essential that all the dynamic contrasts and shapes are confidently conveyed.

At the end, as the parade continues into the distance, there should be no ritardando – just a carefully judged diminuendo and very light, cheekily played final Gs with the disappearance of the last reveller over the hill.

C:6 Slavický *A Czech Song*

Do not be fooled by the complex appearance: repetition abounds in this delightfully witty piece. It is easy to practise and learn, providing that the performer has nimble fingers, a good sense of rhythm and a quick wit. The rhythmic ideas are playful and unpredictable, with laughter springing from the semiquaver/quaver motifs and the joke punch-lines in the accented offbeat chords.

It is helpful to begin with the phrases' rhythmic patterns, working at these in isolation and ensuring that the rhythmic identity of each four-bar phrase is internalized. Good strategies to employ might be clapping against a pulse, making up words, and playing imaginary notes on a table top or piano lid while adding dynamic contrast to maintain a connection with the music.

The more technically challenging motifs of bars 2, 7, 8, 17–18 and 32 can be practised slowly, conditioning the articulation and co-ordination into the fingers. It is important to be conscientious about the finger-changes on the repeated notes as well as using the pedal where marked, in order to enhance the phrasing.

A confident sense of performance will be needed, since hesitation or lack of rhythmic precision will destroy the humour. In the earlier stages it is worth playing the piece through a few times, focusing on the tempo, articulation and rhythmic character, allowing notes to take second place; this will build the mental agility to think ahead while playing. Slow practice, putting the detail back in later, will pay dividends.

This suits a spontaneous extrovert, since it requires a more creative dynamic range than marked to energize the phrases as well as bold execution of the detail. The piece will reward all the hard work, and giving it a strong, flamboyant ending will bring audiences to their feet.

GRADE 5

Forward planning will be especially helpful when preparing for Grade 5. Around this time students often find that other commitments compete with their piano practice time. The inclusion of some light pieces that are quick to learn will help to maintain enjoyment in playing, while the exam work is being systematically covered.

A:1 J. S. Bach *Prelude in C minor*

This Prelude is a perfect example of Bach's genius in composing miniatures for developing keyboard players. One can imagine his delight in producing the new manuscript during a lesson, perhaps for one of his own sons, with confidence that it will inspire many hours of absorbing practice.

Despite the title, it has a clear dance feel and will encourage the ability to create musical beauty out of an almost constant line of quavers. An unhurried but flowing tempo will best capture the music's grace and gentle expressive mood. Although Bach generally left no musical instructions detailed on his scores, players should feel free to convey the phrasing and harmonic progress through well-varied dynamics. For this piece, a range of *pianissimo* to *mezzo-forte* should encompass both the tender moments and those of a richer colouring.

Carefully planned articulation will also be important in giving the music vitality. Although the left-hand crotchets may at first appear to be accompaniment, there are many places where they form a melodic duet with the upper (or occasionally lower) right-hand quavers. Obvious examples are bars 5–8 and 13–15; the bass could be kept legato, with the rising right-hand outline brought out as a third voice. Repeating right-hand quavers should be as soft as possible, to avoid intruding. Elsewhere, many of the crotchets could be detached, or partly slurred, to find interest and elegance.

The three-in-a-bar character will suggest a lightening of second and third beats, but the Baroque feature of hemiola creates rhythmic interest in bars 38–9. The two rising right-hand 7th arpeggios introduce this, with the second of them giving importance to the third beat of bar 38. The second and third beats of bar 39 form the Prelude's closing cadence, with the stress coming mid-bar.

Pedal would not be helpful in this clean-textured music. However, even fingerwork and singing tone will lay good foundations for shaping both individual phrases and the overall architectural design.

A:2 J. L. Dussek *Allegro non tanto*

Happy, effervescent pieces are surprisingly rare, but this sunny Sonatina movement would make a popular contribution to a small concert, as well as being great fun to learn. Circus clowns on bicycles would provide a colourful image to characterize the strong forward momentum and teasing dynamic contrasts.

A precautionary *non tanto* warns against reckless velocity. The running semiquavers will need some slow and careful preparation to ensure precision and even tone when fluency is achieved. The notes lie comfortably under the fingers for all but the smallest hands, so a good fingering plan should lead to security in performance. Extra attention may be needed to choose suitable fingering for the repeated 6ths at the change of bars 1–2. A flexible wrist and subtle shifting of hand weight will be helpful for neatness. Applying the same technique for the recurring Alberti bass patterns will ensure that tension does not creep in when a more rapid tempo is attempted.

Elsewhere, the examiner will appreciate crisp, light staccatos in most left-hand quavers. If the student likes, some of the right-hand quavers could also be detached, to give lightness at the end of bars 3, 17 and 19, for example. Short phrases (the slurred pairs in bars 2–3, rising/falling groups in bars 5–6 and 31–3, and the zany patterns in bars 17–20) could benefit from a sinking wrist where full right-hand tone is wanted, and a slightly lifted wrist where phrases/pairs finish lightly. Care might be needed to avoid accenting notes that follow long, dying-away ones (e.g. second note of bars 5 and 17). However, the syncopated second note in bar 7 could enjoy a playful rhythmic nudge, as could the minims of the main theme.

Balance between the hands for the repeating left-hand quavers will require a listening ear, so that they contribute forward motion without becoming heavy. A moment of ritenuto before the theme's return and a well-controlled diminuendo in the last bar might add irresistible final touches of humour.

A:3 I. J. Pleyel *Adagio*

A remarkable feature of this Adagio by Pleyel is that it is almost entirely major in tonality. The consequent smiling mood is combined with warm 6ths and 3rds, to create music of charm and contentment. No grey clouds here to remind us of the worries in life!

Although the music has quite a busy appearance on the page, frequent rests and staccatos result in short moments of complete silence. These need to be enjoyed for their particular effect with the temptation to hurry forwards to the next sound resisted. There are a few tricky rhythmic features, particularly the quicker notes in bars 14–15, some of which must be played between semiquavers. The image of a small bird fluttering might allow these to decorate the ensuing note, while maintaining a steady pulse. In exam performances the first-time bar will not actually be played until the end of the da capo, since repeats are not required. The line should initially conclude with the second-time bar, which needs to be counted carefully to avoid shortening the rest.

Patient slow practice of ornaments will help integrate them into the melodic line without undue accents. The suggested realizations work well, but it will be necessary to keep in mind the unornamented melody to pre-serve the music's rhythmic poise. Especially hazardous is the middle of bar 2, where hurrying into the ornament would unsettle the pulse.

The soaring melody is accompanied by a mostly reticent left hand, whose chords in bars 1–3 could be lightly lifted to match the right-hand staccatos (shown by wedges). Left-hand articulation elsewhere often offers the player free choice, as there are few markings. The music could be either noble and expansive or gently dancing, according to the articulation and dynamic choices made. A subtle touch of pedal, here and there, might add warmth. Above all, musical phrasing and a singing tone will allow the melody to rise and fall with joy.

A:4 Handel *Entrée in G minor*

'Entrée', meaning the start of a group of dances and songs, was a term used in eighteenth-century *opéra-ballet*. A sense of elegance and momentum will capture the idea of theatrical display in this sparkling piece.

Articulation skills will be to the fore in a successful performance. Groups of quavers might gain vitality from a gentle slurring from first to second note in each four, with the remaining three lightly staccato. Other options, each giving their own character, are equally acceptable. Semiquaver runs require neat finger precision to maintain an even and bright tone; well-rounded hands, with fingertips kept close to the keys, will help to ensure this. Musical shaping of these runs will prevent a relentless feel from creeping into the patterns. The rising sequences in bar 3 and bars 10–11 can also grow in volume as they reach the top, but should not approach *fortissimo*. A relaxed *forte* will keep the music within its natural scope.

The imitation after the double bar is an opportunity to develop skilful independence of the hands. The first two notes of each hand, and their step down each a beat later, will need extra brightness; in-between notes can retire to the background. Other engaging changes of mood include the modulation to the relative major in bar 3; this might be reflected in a more gentle touch, before the brilliant scales in bar 4. A slight cloud passes across the sunshine at the start of bar 6; a more legato feel could express this touchingly.

Cadences, particularly important in Baroque music, present a sense of gathering together and should have a quite definite robustness. A moment could be taken to establish the new key in the middle of bar 12, before the left hand's moment of glory to follow. The right hand's chords should be quite reticent here, until its own joyous theme takes over in bar 14. There is another enjoyable moment as bar 18 arrives, and the subdominant harmony could be briefly 'placed' before the music's final flourish.

A:5 Haydn *Minuet in C minor*

Despite the serious mood and frequent rests of the opening bars, this memorable Minuet has a delightfully tuneful quality. Snatches of it might return to mind at any moment, long after the piano lid has been closed!

The examiner will be listening for a cantabile right-hand tone and elegantly shaped phrases. Careful attention to all markings will be needed, especially to convey the searching feel of bars 23–30. The left hand in bars 18–21 would benefit from the technical work of practising the quavers separately from the crotchets to guide proper co-ordination. All left-hand accompaniments will need to be kept light, so that the melody sings out.

The surprise harmony in bar 11 signals modulation to a sunnier key. Brief touches of pedal would warm the tone here, but the right-hand paired articulation needs clarity in the second half of any pedalled bars. The first section ends with characteristically Haydnesque wit. The right hand's minims should be resonant but not heavy, and crisp acciaccaturas will bring a smile to any listeners.

Further harmonic beauty comes in the last section; this is one of Haydn's most inspired passages. Students may enjoy discovering how he achieves these twists to the expected flow, touching on D♭ major in bar 44 and colouring the chords of bars 39 and 45. (Any E♭s in bar 39, left hand, should be played E♮, following Haydn's original.) The coda passage of bars 47–51 would be effective if given light legato pedalling, lifting as each new beat sounds and replacing immediately. This will first need slow practice, to ensure that right-hand quavers are not too smudged and that rests are silent above the tonic bass notes. The remaining bars should be crisply articulated and *a tempo*, with tenuto and staccato marks carefully observed.

This apparently unassuming-looking dance develops into a jewel of piano music, given a sense of curiosity and discovery in the performer. It is a wonderful introduction to Haydn's compositions.

A:6 Mozart *Allegro*

This is a happy, ebullient piece, much in the style of Mozart's wind serenades and early symphonies. Pairs or groups of instruments can frequently be imagined taking centre-stage, with the different tonal colours adding drama.

Early preparation should include the double 3rds and 6ths in each hand, so that the notes are perfectly co-ordinated. In bars 10–13 the right hand could be thought of as two flutes, with as smooth and singing a legato line as possible, despite the restless left-hand articulation. In bars 32–5 the left hand may also present a challenge in keeping together and quiet; a slight lean on the outer side of the hand – and care taken to retain the thumb close to the keys – will avoid distracting attention from the melody above.

Subtle use of the pedal in the minim bars, replacing it directly after each note-change, adds warmth to the sparse texture. Bars 50 and 66 would also be enhanced by pedalling across the crotchet beats, with care taken to avoid harmonic smudging. A touch of pedal on the minims of bars 40 and 44 could add piquancy to these expressive notes.

Only *forte* and *piano* dynamic markings appear, but much elegance can be created by adding shape within these markings. Falling phrases will benefit from a diminuendo. Rising ones, especially those leading to a dissonance (e.g. the start of bars 28 and 30), can be given a smoothly graded crescendo, with any subsequent resolution allowed to fall away. Firm fingertips and flexible forearm weight will give resonance on loud notes, avoiding harshness.

The imitative passage in bars 51–4 is especially striking, and the incisiveness of the syncopated notes contrasts with the smooth-flowing quavers. Oboe and bassoon could be at work here, perhaps. The first phrase, in the major key, is bold and optimistic; sensitivity to the minor inflection of the second will bring an extra dimension to this predominantly cheerful piece.

B:1 J. F. F. Burgmüller *L'orage (The Storm)*

Burgmüller is certainly a master of the attractive, pictorial study and this musical depiction of a storm provides 'Liszt-for-the-learner' material. It has the added allure of sounding harder than it is.

Despite its obvious drama, the piece is a study and develops technical skills: principal among these being forearm rotation to master the tremolos; these mostly feature octave spans but sometimes smaller intervals as well. The technique requires a smooth, even action from a relaxed forearm and wrist, with the rotation being restrained rather than extravagant and close enough to the keyboard to maintain tonal control. Where crescendos and diminuendos are marked, forearm weight can be gradually increased and then decreased. In places such as bars 9 and 11 the right-hand semiquavers can be practised by playing the first two notes together (as a 3rd, 4th or 5th) and then the second two notes (as an octave) so as to gauge the distances involved. However it is also important, at an early stage, to establish precisely the timing of these semiquavers in relation to those in the left hand.

For the stormy picture to be conveyed, dynamic projection is very important. *Pianissimo* levels can be aided by the *una corda* pedal and hairpins should if anything be over- rather than under-played. The *fortissimo* in bars 13 and 14 needs real power, especially from the left hand, so considerable arm weight should be engaged by dropping down from well above the keyboard. Some pedalling is marked in the copy but its use is desirable elsewhere, for example in bars 7, 15 and 16a, and from bar 20 (where the major tonality suggests that the storm is receding). Clarity must however be achieved in places such as bars 1 and 18 where pedal use may be less appropriate.

A tempo of crotchet = *c.*126 should be manageable by most students at this level, although for the more agile ones, crotchet = 138 will add extra excitement – as long as control and musicality is preserved!

B:2 Glier *Gaiamente*

With its interesting rhythms and melodic charms, this piece is typical of its Russian composer. If your student has not previously encountered a 5/4 time signature, it may be helpful to think of the bars as two beats plus three beats, as the footnote suggests. The most frequently repeated rhythm is that which occurs in bar 3 (which sounds out all five beats of the bar), so practising this rhythm first before matching up the rest is a good start. The tempo needs to be *gaiamente* ('gaily') and the suggested minim = *c*.92 is appropriate but, as minims do not fit into a 5/4 bar, it will be easier to think of the tempo as crotchet = *c*.184, however off-puttingly fast this may seem!

Despite its rhythmic challenges, the piece is primarily melodic, so upper right-hand notes should be gently leaned on for the required projection. Thinking in phrases may also help. These are of variable lengths: for example, four bars (at the opening), two bars (at bars 19–20), five bars (at bars 5–9), and even six bars (at bars 31–6). Identifying these and allowing them their natural musical contouring will help to give the piece shape and direction. The character of the music is also revealed through the dynamics, many of which are shown as *mezzo-forte* and above. However, these need to be viewed in the context of a Romantic miniature so, to preserve a singing tone, *forte* levels can be achieved mostly by finger pressure – though the forearm will need some firmness too.

For added resonance the pedal should be used where specifically indicated but, to avoid textural patchiness, it should be applied throughout, with the harmonic changes, as delineated by the bass, guiding the foot. It is therefore appropriate to change the pedal on the third beat of bar 29 and equivalent places.

Glier remains silent concerning the subject of his sketch, but your student may well have some ideas!

B:3 H. Hofmann *Am Abend (In the Evening)*

It is hard to imagine a lovelier 'song without words' than this Schumann-esque evocation of the evening.

Crucial here is a singing tone and textural balance, so the musical layers can be prioritized. Leaning into the uppermost notes by very slightly tilting the forearm rightwards will aid melodic projection. Since this technique requires some underpinning by the bass notes, the left hand will need enough depth of touch to support but not to dominate. The inner right-hand quavers should be heard, but no more than the merest finger weight is needed for audibility to be achieved in the correct proportion. Where the left hand has the melody (as in bars 17–20) adjustments will be needed, bearing in mind that low-register melodies – here perhaps imitating a tenor voice – usually need more help from the performer than their treble counterparts.

This piece is very lyrical, so singing aloud the melodies is a good way of feeling the phrasing and allowing metaphorical breathing to occur when playing. Most phrases are four bars long, but occasionally there is an eight-bar phrase (as at bars 9–16) where the music bespeaks a longer structure, despite the slurs marked in the copy. The music needs a gentle momentum (dotted crotchet = *c*.80, or even a few degrees slower, is suitable), but subtle rubato can be introduced at phrase-ends (e.g. bar 8, bars 15–16).

Quite a big dynamic range is indicated (*pianissimo* up to *forte*), but the sound always needs warmth so hitting the piano to achieve *forte* should be avoided; the *una corda* pedal can be reserved for the last chord. Use of the sustaining pedal throughout – not only where marked – will enhance the necessary tonal richness. Changes often synchronize with the beat, but the harmonies are, as usual, the determining factor.

This piece will provide a pleasant point of repose in a Grade 5 programme – and playing it to family or friends would also be a lovely way to end an evening.

B:4 Bridge *Allegretto con moto*

This delightfully whimsical piece may seem on the long side for this grade, but given that much of the material in the first half of the piece is later repeated (albeit an octave higher), in reality there is only about a page-and-a-half of music to learn.

Perhaps at an *allegretto* tempo of crotchet = *c*.92–100 the touch can often be lightly detached; practising can therefore focus on the sensation of the finger leaving rather than entering the key. Motions must be economical if the predominantly *piano*/*pianissimo* dynamic levels are to be maintained. Even where the music rises to *mezzo-forte*, it might be helpful to think of this as a generous *mezzo-piano*. Pedalling is generally unnecessary, although its use in bar 24 and similar passages will add some welcome warmth to the sound; the touch can also be deeper and more sustained. The jumping 6ths (and one tritone) in bars 29–30 and 37–8 present a more specifically technical challenge and they can be practised as block chords.

The last quaver of bar 29 and the first of 30 can then be practised in isolation to instil the size of the leap still further into both mind and muscle. Memorizing these bars might also be helpful because both visual and kinaesthetic senses are engaged.

Much of the piece falls into four-bar phrases. For example, it might be helpful to think of the opening phrase as subtly peaking on the first beat of bar 3 and slightly dying away during bar 4. At bar 9 the music falls more naturally into two-bar phrases which, allied to the *mezzo-forte* indication, suggests a more animated feeling – though with no hint of rushing. Careful observation of rests in the later stages of the piece adds to the character of the music, and where Bridge has written *ten.* (tenuto) the effect can be quite pronounced, especially in the context of *Lento*, otherwise the examiner may not notice it!

B:5 Jensen *Lied (Song)*

In this Lied (song) the right hand does the singing, so achieving a good textural balance is crucial for a successful performance. It may be helpful to think of the left-hand part as at least one dynamic level lower than the right: where the music is marked *forte*, for instance, the left-hand semi-quavers will provide all the necessary harmonic support if they are played at no more than a healthy *mezzo-piano*, using finger weight rather than arm weight. The singing tone will need to be maintained when the right-hand part goes into double notes (at bar 37) so practising with the arm and hand tilted very slightly towards the fifth finger will help to preserve the distinctive melodic colour of the upper voice.

The printed ABRSM metronome mark is appropriately slow but if the music moves slightly faster (crotchet = *c.*56) the flow remains unhurried and might enhance the phrasing. The music is constructed in four-bar phrases, and awareness of this can inform how the dynamic contours indicated in the score may be interpreted. Despite the *mezzo-forte* marking at the start, the phrase seems to peak naturally at the high B in bar 4 and then subside quite rapidly.

The dynamic markings range from *pianissimo* to *forte*, though here *forte* can probably imply 'full' rather than 'loud'. However, to achieve the steep drop from the opening *mezzo-forte* to the *pianissimo* in bar 2, exaggeration may be a helpful practice strategy. By opening very loudly, your student will create more scope for a rapid diminuendo and, once the effect is mastered, the volume levels can be adjusted for greater subtlety and musicality. Pedalling is needed and changing with each beat will work most of the time, although there are places where more frequent changes are desirable, such as in bars 21–3.

Nowadays, a piece of non-vocal music is often referred to as a 'song' so here is a piece of piano music where the reference is indeed appropriate!

B:6 Maikapar *Prelude in F*

The opening of this piece is like a prelude to a prelude; the first four bars have an improvisatory feeling, as if the pianist is finding his or her way to the main prelude which commences at bar 5. These opening bars can therefore be played quite freely (and more leisurely than the ensuing *Andantino con moto*), though not to the extent that all sense of time and metre is suspended.

Once underway, the right-hand part needs plenty of tonal warmth, a rich cantabile from firm but pliant fingers. It is helpful to take note primarily of the long phrase-marks because preoccupation with more localized slurring could result in a fussy and disjointed effect. The right hand's accompanying two-note chords on beats 2 and 4 in places such as bar 8 and, especially, bar 10 need to be kept well out of the way and could judiciously be marked *pianissimo*. Left-hand choreography, describing a series of elegant curves, coaxing rather than hitting the keys, can also aid the textural balance. Pedalling will enhance the texture and can be applied mostly on a bar-by-bar basis except in bar 22 and, possibly, bars 27–29 where it will need to be changed with every minim. The *una corda* pedal can helpfully be engaged from bar 30 to the end but its use at the beginning of the piece, despite the printed instruction, seems questionable.

The loudest marked dynamic is *mezzo-piano*, although observing the hairpins will take the volume a little higher in places. Intimacy is implied but the dynamic nuances must be sufficiently projected for the examiner to be made aware of them. It may therefore sometimes be necessary to play with a little more weight than one might at first imagine.

The printed metronome marks certainly keep the music flowing, but if the *Andantino con moto* is taken at crotchet = *c*.126, extra space is allowed and the music can perhaps breathe a little more. This is definitely a piece for the more sensitive pianist.

C:1 Bartók *Este a székelyeknél (An Evening in the Village)*

Sometimes known as 'Evening in Transylvania' (Székely land), this is a piece that Bartók loved and often played himself. The region of Eastern Transylvania is very beautiful, its villages nestling in the valleys with the Carpathian Mountains beyond; Bartók knew the area well.

The piece is in ABABA form, with the repetitions subjected to variation. The two Hungarian folk melodies used are pentatonic and are contrasted by tempo and mood. The first is in *parlando* style, so it would be helpful to imagine it sung; your student might like to invent some words to fit. It is evident from Bartók's own recordings that he treats this melody very freely. However, it is important to observe the differences in the length of the melody's first note wherever it appears, as well as the changes in metre.

The second melody is a dance, and here Bartók asks for it to be played in strict time. At both its appearances it is playful but quiet, as though being heard from a distance or recalled like a memory. The original folk-dance might have been played on a peasant flute or violin, and in its second appearance (bar 30) the added decorative figures are typical of Magyar music. Bartók gives all the musical directions that are needed, and all dynamics and articulation marks should be meticulously observed. Metronome marks are also the composer's; Bartók was very particular about tempo – sometimes even indicating exactly how long a piece should last!

Extra pedal may be added sparingly to give sonority to longer notes or chords, but the pedal marks that are given in the score are very important and must be applied exactly as shown. In bars 18–19 and 38–40 the accompanying chords should still be played staccato but lightly. In the second of these passages the pedal creates a haunting effect rather like bird-calls echoing across the valley. This is surely a piece to be cherished.

C:2 Tansman *Cache-cache (Hide-and-Seek)*

The music of Polish-born composer Alexandre Tansman is probably best known to guitarists, but he wrote prolifically for most genres. It is interesting to note that his second piano concerto was dedicated to Charlie Chaplin. The four volumes of *Pour les enfants* contain some delightful character pieces, and this one will be great fun, especially for the extrovert performer.

It will be important to avoid tension at all stages of learning and playing. Note-repetition and the type of attack required can be tiring if the player is not frequently reminded to keep arms and wrists loose. The left hand's repeated quavers are best played with hand (wrist) staccato, the arm held a little higher than usual. Lightly tapping on a flat surface, watching how the hand drops easily from the wrist, is a good starting-point. Only a small movement will be required, and, once back at the piano, forcing the tone at *forte* level should be avoided. The *martellato* accents of the right-hand melody (bar 2 and similar) must be marked strongly, with a tiny break before each one adding impetus to the syncopation.

If the first three repeated Cs in bar 17 are played with fingers 1-3-2, a sequence of 1-4-3-2 can follow which conveniently places the thumb on the first quaver of each group. The same fingering can be used by the left hand in bars 20–1. In bars 30–3 the descending bass line may be played by alternating fingers 3 and 4 until arriving on 5 for the lowest note. These lower notes should be practised first, passing finger 3 over 4 to create a legato line. This will act as a foil to the right hand's slurred pairs.

The first section sets the scene, while one can imagine the children hiding in the quieter middle section. The loudest moments must be saved for the last four bars. Here the repeated notes could be played by alternating fingers 1 and 3, creating a virtuosic flourish as the excited children scamper for the 'home-base'.

C:3 Evelien Vis *60s Swing*

The jaunty good humour of this piece will make it a popular choice. The fact that almost half of it is repeated in one way or another is an added bonus for those with a busy schedule!

The swing rhythm is clearly notated in bar 2 and will continue throughout. Only bars with four consecutive crotchets (e.g. bar 6) and minims (e.g. bars 7–8) will sound straight. For students not familiar with swing there are plenty of performances to be heard online. The dynamics are well marked in the score to provide variety, but adding nuances that follow the rise and fall of the phrases will make for a more musical performance.

There is often anxiety about how much pedal to employ. The piece could be played without any pedal at all, but then there is a danger that many of the accompanying minim chords will be too short. To help join the chords in bar 4, for instance, legato pedalling could be used, and then again in bars 6–8 and 12–16, changing with each left-hand chord.

The tempo will eventually be quite fast – it must be felt as two-in-a-bar not four – so a few fingering adjustments might be helpful. Unless the stretch is too wide it will be easier to play the right-hand figure in bar 2 simply with 1-2-3-4-5. There will be no difficulty as long as the arm is allowed to travel laterally behind the fingers. In the middle section when the left hand has the melody, the phrase will flow more comfortably if the right hand takes the crotchet F in bar 18 – the thumb will already be over that note. The same situation occurs in bar 22.

Towards the end, the temptation to slow down too soon must be resisted, and the rallentando reserved for the last two bars. After a carefree character throughout, the music finally comes to rest in a mood of pure contentment.

C:4 Valerie Capers *Sweet Mister Jelly Roll*

Ragtime was all the rage in America from the end of the nineteenth century to the early part of the twentieth, with Jelly Roll Morton one of its most famous exponents. The style was so named because of its ragged rhythm or syncopation.

This affectionate tribute to one of the jazz greats is fun to play and not unduly demanding technically as long as the style is understood. Listening to some recorded ragtime pieces will obviously help. A really firm pulse is required and this is provided by the sturdy left-hand part. It would do no harm to practise this with a metronome. The right hand swaggers and pulls against the beat, with the accents and syncopated notes positively marked. In bar 32 the given fingering suggests that the first chord should also have a B♭, the same as in bar 30.

Few dynamics are given, and in view of the repetition that occurs, it would be sensible to add more. Your student should be encouraged to make suggestions about this. It would also be wise to show where to jump to in the score by using asterisks or colours to mark the repeats; it is quite confusing to the eye otherwise.

The form of the piece has some of the characteristics of a rondo, with the principal theme (A) played three times. The second theme (B) is at bar 9, and the third (C) at bar 29. This last tune only appears once, so for the sake of the piece's structure it would be best to make the repeat.

The piece could be played without pedal, but there are instances where pedal would add to the verve of the rhythm. These include the fourth beat of bar 16 to give impetus to the restart of the melody, the minims in bar 19, and the first crotchet chord in bar 20 to emphasize the syncopation. The tempo is certainly lively, but, as Scott Joplin said, 'It is never right to play ragtime fast'.

C:5 Shande Ding *To the Suburbs*

Suite for Children, by the celebrated Chinese composer Shande Ding, is subtitled *Happy Holidays,* which helps us to understand the mood of each of the five miniatures it contains.

The character of 'To the Suburbs' is made clearer by another translation that calls it 'Outing'. Perhaps the delicate filigree effect of the opening section describes the leafy lanes outside the city centre, and the pleasurable feeling of breathing cleaner air. The livelier middle section suggests games in the park, and raising the metronome speed here to dotted crotchet = 84 would be sufficient for *più animato.* The unmistakable Chinese flavour of the music is created by the use of the pentatonic scale and high tessitura of the instrument.

As the piece is in ternary form, the da capo direction must be observed. Fingering and dynamics are fully provided, but care must be taken to observe all the octave higher lines – the one for the left hand in bar 5 could be missed.

There are no indications given for pedal, but the piece will be greatly enhanced by its use. Initially a change on first beats will suffice, but at bar 6 the change can wait until the rest. In the next passage direct pedalling follows the pattern of the left hand, lifting for the rests. In the middle section, a quick dab of pedal will reinforce the accented chords (bars 16, 20, 29 and 33), and then it is a case of pedalling so that rests and staccato notes can be heard. The most exciting passage starts with the upbeat to bar 24, and here it is possible to pedal right through to each rest, marking the accents firmly. This not only makes it easier to play, but adds sonority and a change of colour.

With the return to the opening section, a mood of contentment pervades as the family wends its way home with happy memories of a day out.

C:6 Shostakovich *Dance*

Ballet, puppetry and the theatre have always been close to the hearts of Russian composers. These delightful pieces, most of them culled from Shostakovich's own ballet suites, are great fun to play.

The doll in this seventh dance of the set is mercurial in character; fleet of foot and full of mischief. Musically it is not in the least complicated, but a nimble right hand is essential. The quavers in the left hand sound best if they are lightly detached, ticking away like a metronome in the background. In the first half of the piece these accompanying notes lie comfortably under the hand, but later there is some jumping to be done. In bars 17–19 and 23–4 the jump can be virtually eliminated if the pairs of notes A and G are played together by the thumb. That leaves only two bars with leaps. If the chords in bars 25–8 seem to trip up your student, it may help to practise first without the top notes (the repeated A) using fingers 5/3, 4/2 so that concentration is focused on that progression.

In the right hand, the slurs placed over groups of four semiquavers do not necessarily mean that there should be tiny breaks between them – there is hardly time to do that anyway. If preferred, the more conventional fingering that places the thumb on the last note of bar 1 will find the hand in position for almost all of the next two bars. A decisive attack is needed for the accented quaver with its acciaccatura wherever they appear, and dropping into the notes with fingers 3 then 5 is both safe and strong.

Dynamics should be varied, but within a modest range. There are opportunities for echo effects, and the 'wrong note' G♯ in bar 20 must be highlighted. No rallentando is needed at the end, but the semiquavers should be allowed to fade away as the dancer runs off-stage and the curtain falls.

GRADE 6

Your student will now have achieved success in Grade 5 Theory, Practical Musicianship or Jazz. At Grade 6, examiners will be looking for musical character, expression and style to be presented with even greater conviction, and technical fluency will be needed to support the successful realization of these ideas.

A:1 J. S. Bach *Sinfonia in G minor*

The Inventions and Sinfonias provide a wonderful introduction to the contrapuntal style of J. S. Bach. This beautiful three-part invention is both challenging and rewarding.

The final performance will depend upon the initial care taken over preparation, and interest can be stimulated by examining how the music has been constructed. A good start would be to look at how many times the principal five-note motif appears, and how and when the leap of an octave changes interval. Other points to be noted are the descending dotted crotchets first heard in bars 2–5 and the two long dominant pedals (bars 24–9 for D minor, and bars 58–64 for G minor). It is the sustaining of these longer notes and balancing of the three voices that present the biggest challenges.

Even before separate hands practice begins, it is worthwhile taking each voice alone to see what adventures it has. However, when moving on to practising the complete right-hand or left-hand part, it is vital that the middle voice's notes are not omitted. Fingering must be carefully arranged in advance and the ability to employ finger substitution will be essential. In bars 49 and 51 it would be easier to take the last quaver of the middle voice into the right hand, which allows more time for the left hand's manoeuvre.

If the suggested trill in bar 9 proves to be a stumbling-block, it can be simplified. Starting on C, the first beat can be made a semiquaver and two demisemiquavers, the second four demisemiquavers and the third a semiquaver (taking the middle voice's G at the same time) followed by the A and B♮ demisemiquavers shown in the score. This fits easily with the left-hand part. The left hand's short trills should present no problem, if played as suggested with the final note synchronized with the semiquaver above.

Dynamics will be determined by the natural rise and fall of the phrasing, and the ending can be magical if coloured sensitively. With a crescendo from bar 55, the music grows in intensity until it begins to fade at bar 61. A brief ritenuto in bar 64 prepares the way for the reprise of the opening bars; this time, it is played quietly as though recalling a tender memory.

A:2 Beethoven *Minuet and Trio*

It is always an exciting moment when beginning to study even a single movement from one of the large-scale works of Beethoven. He made less use of the minuet than his predecessors, and the contrasts between the familiar graceful dance and sudden outbursts of energy are typical of his style and character.

Several passages would benefit from preliminary attention before they become stumbling-blocks. For the rising groups of semiquavers in bars 5–6, your student should start with fingers 4/3 – in the first two groups tucking the thumb under on the third note – as this will keep the hand in a good position. Co-ordination could be a problem with the semiquaver flourishes that begin in bars 8 and 12, and also in the closing bars of the Minuet where the right hand has to take notes from the bass stave. Slow practice and playing in different rhythms will help the fingers become more disciplined.

Pedal will add warmth to the tone and heighten dynamic effects, but it must be applied carefully. For instance, it could be used from first to third beat in the opening bar and to slurred chords such as those in bars 4 and 14–16. There is a good case for using pedal to underpin the dominant pedal in bars 5–7, depressing the pedal just after the second beat of bars 5–6 and holding it until the end of each tie. A legato change can be made on the second beat of bar 7 but the pedal must be released for the third beat. To avoid the texture becoming muddy the first semiquaver group should be kept light with a positive crescendo made through to the top of the phrase. In bars 9 and 13, pedal applied from the second beat will help build the excitement towards the *fortissimo* chord (which also needs a touch of pedal).

Diligent left-hand work will be needed for the fiery Trio section; practising in different rhythms will help greatly. Tone should not be forced for the scurrying semiquavers; it is the right-hand chords that carry the *sforzandi* and create the drama. The return (da capo) to the Minuet restores a calmer mood and completes this fine movement.

A:3 J. L. Krebs *Allegro*

The cheerful character and uncomplicated texture will make this a popular choice. It requires a lively attack and agile right hand, but is otherwise relatively undemanding.

Repetition plays a large part in the piece, so it would be advisable to employ plenty of dynamic interest. Dynamic marks are scarce with just the occasional *piano* and *forte* – which suggests it was written for a two-manual harpsichord – but when played on the modern piano there is scope and indeed the necessity for more variety to prevent it from becoming monotonous. For instance, the cadences are often repeated (see bars 3–4 and 7–8 and similar) so an echo effect would work well. A variant of the main theme appears in the dominant (bar 9) and two bars later is repeated in the tonic, which gives another opportunity for a quieter level of sound. At bar 13 the rising sequential passage invites a crescendo. Similar ideas can be applied throughout the piece, and your student should be encouraged to make suggestions.

Repeated notes are also a feature – sadly, this often encourages players to dig into the key and produce shapeless phrasing. Usually a row of repeated notes should either increase or decrease in volume to provide contour and interest. In the first two bars of the principal theme, a slight swelling towards the middle of the bar will provide momentum and shape. The left hand has a typical continuo type of accompaniment. Therefore, it may help to imagine it played on the cello, with the bow lightly bouncing off the string.

The character of the music suggests that most quavers should be staccato. Some slurs are given in the score, but there are a few other places where they would add expression. These are in bars 7, 8, 35 and 36 where first and third beats could be slurred. The given realizations for the cadential trills may prove difficult to fit in without slowing down, so they may be adapted. In bars 3, 24, 27, 31 and 44, the eight notes could be reduced to six and those that begin with an appoggiatura could use the pattern realized at bar 20. A tempo of crotchet = *c.*84 should be enough to convey the joyful, extrovert mood.

A:4 J. C. F. Bach *Allegro in B flat*

Friedrich, as he was called to distinguish him from all the other Johanns in the family, was the ninth son of J. S. Bach, and one of several who achieved eminence as both a composer and performer. This Allegro is not particularly demanding technically, but it will need a confident and lively attack with a metronome speed of crotchet = *c*.112.

Choice of articulation must be the first consideration. Most of the quavers and crotchets will sound best detached, although crotchets need to be held a little longer. However, slurs will act as accents in appropriate places. In the principal theme, for instance, it would be effective to slur B♭ to F in the first bar and C to F in the second. This is then imitated by the left hand. A nuance up to and away from the middle of these opening bars will add shape and immediately establish the feeling of two beats in a bar. A slur from the dotted crotchet to the second quaver in bars 5, 6 and 7 will shift the accent back to the first beat of the bar, while in bars 14 and 30 slurring the tied notes over to the last quaver will highlight the syncopation there.

The next consideration should be the fingering. In the Editio Musica Budapest version, the fingering is detailed, but it relies a great deal on placing the fifth finger on black keys. This works very well as long as the hand is tilted towards the black key in good time. The thumb is more commonly placed on black notes. However in bar 30, it would be better to use fingers 4-2-1-2, in order to avoid a rather awkward shift in the third group of semiquavers.

Finally, decisions will have to be made about dynamics. In accordance with the practice of the day, the piece should begin *forte*, but a diminuendo could start at bar 5 to arrive at *piano* by about bar 11. The music continues to rise and fall, either gradually or stepwise with the sequences; starting *piano* in bar 24 (at the turn towards F minor), it can build gradually towards a joyful ending.

A:5 Mozart *Allegro*

Most aspiring pianists will eventually try their hand at Mozart's so-called 'Sonata Facile'. Despite its length, it is bound to be a popular choice.

It is vital that the tempo is maintained from section to section; one of the most common mistakes is to start too fast and then slow down for the semiquaver passages. Even when practising slowly, the correct relationship between crotchets and semiquavers should be preserved. This movement will provide a wonderful opportunity to develop the various types of touch that Mozart's music needs.

A beautiful singing tone is required for the purely melodic material found in the opening four bars of the first subject, and again for the second subject which begins in bar 14. The accompanying figures to these melodies will need a lighter touch, with the fingers kept close to the keys. For the scales that form the bridge passage (bars 5–12) your student should be encouraged to employ a light, slightly higher finger attack in order to produce a clearly articulated stream of notes. Once the notes are familiar, a good method of practice is to play on the surface of the keys listening to the light tapping of the fingers. This 'upper key-noise' is what creates the slight separation of each note sometimes described as *jeu perlé*. Other semiquaver passages could have a more brilliant attack, such as those in the second theme of the second subject group (bars 18–25) and the closing bars of the exposition that follow.

Many players struggle with long cadential trills. Slow practice with hands together is a start, keeping the trill perfectly even. Practising the last beat of the trill (with its turned ending) at different speeds, finishing neatly on the first beat of the next bar, is another useful ploy. Depending on the edition being used, there may be no dynamic marks in the score. Nuances that follow the rise and fall of the phrasing will give shape, and there is scope for echo effects in places. In the development section, the minor keys may suggest different colours, and the arrival into the subdominant key for the recapitulation (bar 42) is a surprise worth highlighting in some way.

A:6 Telemann *Fuga seconda*

At first glance this delightful piece might seem too slight a composition to be called a fugue. However, it is quite tightly constructed and should be examined prior to any serious practice in order to ensure a convincing interpretation. The subject is announced in the right hand – a bright and breezy theme. This is answered by the left hand in the dominant key of E major, accompanied by a quaver figure that may be described as the countersubject and closely related to the subject. It appears with four out of the eight statements of the subject and is easily recognized by its staccato marks.

The subject always begins on the second quaver beat of the bar and, after its initial statements, returns in bars 8 and 11 (unusually both times in the same voice). It then appears at bars 27 and 29 in D major, overlapping as though in *stretto*, and is overlapping again in bars 43 and 45 but now back in the tonic.

The first section ends in F♯ minor with a strong cadence employing the hemiola (bars 21–2) – a rhythmic device much loved by Baroque composers. It will strengthen the rhythm here if the left-hand quavers are slurred in pairs, and the trills above played from their upper notes as four demisemiquavers. A similar cadence is found in bars 32 and 33 in D major.

Apart from the subject itself, the fugue is full of short motifs which are tossed from hand to hand – the descending group of semiquavers and octave leap (bars 14–15), for instance. Of even more significance is the figure that is first heard in the right hand of bars 20–1: the descending semi-quavers that then rise through a chord shape and end with a quaver. This motif is employed teasingly in the last eight bars of the fugue: first in the right hand; then, after a silence, in the left; and finally, after another rest, played triumphantly in the right hand again. Using dynamic contrasts of *forte, piano* and *forte* for these phrases will make for an exciting ending. A metronome speed of dotted crotchet = *c*.56 will give the music sufficient scope to sparkle.

B:1 Bortkiewicz *Erster Schmerz (First Sorrow)*

Although this composer's name will be unfamiliar to many, his music is immediately accessible and will give pleasure to players and listeners alike. The indication *doloroso* gives the clue; feelings of loss and loneliness can be explored as the sorrow of the title finds expression. Pianists who enjoy imagining a storyline will find plenty to inspire their playing in this piece.

Relatively well-developed hands will be an advantage here. Some chords have wide spacing, with both melody and accompaniment included in each hand. The ability to create a warm tone will make the most of many rich harmonies. For example, your student will need to experiment with the chords in bar 6 in order to find the best combination of wrist and arm weight; a good balance of arm relaxation with firmness at the fingertips will produce optimum warmth.

Careful layering of the different voices will help bring the texture to life. In bars 1–5, the left-hand thumb plays a secondary melodic role under the main right-hand tune. These left-hand tenor notes will need greater weight than the chords around them. The dissonant ones should have extra meaning and weight (the C on the third beat of bar 4 and the B on the first beat of bar 5), with ensuing notes resolving tension expressively. The top note in the middle of bar 22 (right-hand, tied middle C, written in the bass clef) should be carefully placed, as it becomes dissonant in the next bar. If its sound has already disappeared by the new bar, the clash with the E dominant 7th below will not be established.

Indications for legato pedalling are marked. Bortkiewicz included many musical instructions, notably at the increasingly anguished bars 13–15. Attentive listening and carefully weighted touch will prevent these accents becoming harsh in tone. The quiet chords in the last bar could present a challenge on an unfamiliar piano, so this would be an important bar to try out before any exam or performance. Whether the player feels this bar as a point of comforting resolution or one of despair, the chords will need a confident touch to capture effectively the *pianissimo* marking. A sense of relaxing into the chords will help avoid an uneven (or silent) tone.

B:2 Chopin *Mazurka in C*

The chance to play Chopin's music is always a treat for developing pianists. A few of his pieces have relatively straightforward notes, as in this Mazurka, and the musical journey in discovering their expressive depths is inspiring.

The marking *Semplice* (simply) could be rather misleading, as there is much musical detail to be mastered before it will be at all simple to play! The chromatic melodic inflections and the modulation to A♭ major in the middle will require sensitivity to tonal colouring. A dramatic moment is the start of the middle section, where surprise D♭ minor chords sweep away any earlier sense of sunny contentment. A slightly quicker tempo at this point would give the section spirit and energy.

The harmonies of this Mazurka emphasize the second of each three beats. The amount of emphasis in any bar may depend on one or even several features: the piquancy of the harmony, the melodic position, the rhythmic flow, or the overall structural shape. The implied accents (some are given as editorial suggestions in the ABRSM edition) will need a nudge or lean, rather than any sharp stress. In fact, a momentary sense of rhythmic stretching will often capture the effect more compellingly, with the end of the bar allowed to fall forwards into the next one. This rhythmic flexibility helps to create a sense of phrase, as the rolling motion gathers momentum. A compensatory breathing-space, as phrases end, will prevent the music from having a rushed character.

There are occasional markings on the score for pedal and they suggest that a little melodic blurring is intended. Elsewhere, pedal is left to the player's discretion; legato pedal (changing just as a new beat is sounded) is needed once or twice in each bar, and harmonic smudging should be avoided. The right-hand melody line needs clear projection, using the most cantabile tone that the pianist can develop, and some expressive variety in the A section return would enhance its many beauties.

Of course, bringing all these technical ideas together to support the player's artistic vision will be far from simple. However, the examiner will be listening for a natural simplicity of communication, with musical phrasing and a sense of dance.

B:3 Grieg *Liten fugl (Little Bird)*

Grieg's enchanting portrait of a little bird offers scope for an imaginative approach. The piece has an exciting, mysterious feel and its sound-world is enticing. It would suit a player who has a light, nimble touch, but could also be an excellent opportunity to encourage agility and precision in a player of more robust playing style.

Neat, crisp fingerwork should ensure sparkle in the demisemiquavers. The manner of approaching and leaving the keys, for each flutter-group of four fast notes and a staccato, is important in maintaining a dancing rhythm. It will benefit from a slight lifting of the wrist from the staccato note, to give looseness to the movement, with a light drop on to the next group. Not all the accents are marked at the same point in each group, so this movement will vary according to where the weight is most needed. Wherever the accents fall they should be precise rather than heavy, in order to avoid distorting the character.

Having acquired a feeling for this technique, your student may find that the hands are playing the fast notes at different rates. Co-ordination will best be gained by hands-separate work, beginning with the weaker hand. When reliability is gained at a slower tempo, both hands can aim for equal clarity. The tempo may be gradually increased, with the lift/drop motion incorporated.

Although the *pianissimo* before bar 9 signals a more mysterious mood, the left hand now has the main line and it is important to project its notes with sufficient depth of tone. The accidentals in bars 13–16 look complicated but may be made easier to understand by practising the staccato chords first in order to give a sense of harmonic direction. This phrase should gather forward momentum, avoiding any hint of choppiness. Once an ability to feel musical direction has been uncovered here, the same momentum will be effective in many parts of the piece, where tiny fragments need to flow as a group, as if flying.

The chirruping rhythmic figure (semiquaver slurred to quaver) is an inspired feature which Grieg uses to tie the music together, both in the accompaniment and at cadences. A subtle keyboard touch here will present the music with a sense of wit and delicacy.

B:4 Grovlez *Le pastour*

For an imaginative pianist this gentle lament will offer happy hours spent discovering unfamiliar sounds and attractive modal harmonies. It may also be a first opportunity to play in a free rhythmic style, giving a sensation of creating the music afresh at each performance.

The piece is based on a French poem, so perhaps there needs to be a little help in translation, to inspire musical thoughts. The images encompass an enchanted forest, a spring, water trickling, and a lovelorn shepherd singing sadly about a shepherdess.

Loose, flexible wrists will ensure enough finger fluidity to capture the transparent tone quality of the improvised hand-crossing arpeggio sections. Rhythmic freedom may be explored adventurously here, using the notated rhythms as an approximate guide; phrase-ends can slow and die away. Encouragement to vary the pacing occasionally during practice may help release a sense of improvisation.

By contrast, the sad melodies of sections such as bars 5–14 will need a firmer cantabile touch, with careful balance between the shapely soprano line and the occasionally contrapuntal lines beneath. A true legato independence of parts is essential here, so early preparation should include work without the pedal, with careful fingering.

As the melody dissolves into a more improvisatory mood (bars 8–12) one might envisage a lyre or guitar being strummed in the left-hand chords. These should be arpeggiated starting at the bar-line, not before it, so that the pedal can comfortably be changed to include the lowest note. Overall, pedal changes can match new harmonies or melodic outline; practising with just left hand and pedal will help to ensure legato pedalling. A little unavoidable smudging of harmonies in bars 1–5 will contribute effectively to the impressionistic tonal colouring. In bar 6 pedal changes on each beat could be considered, but with care taken to hold the minims and the left-hand F into the ensuing crotchets. A brief lift of the pedal before bar 7, and occasionally elsewhere, could help the phrases to breathe.

A feeling at all times of either growing or relaxing (especially tricky in the shaping of repeated notes) should allow these expressive phrases of uneven length to convey the poem's sweet mournfulness.

B:5 Schumann *Thema mit Variationen*

Some music has the power to touch the player's or listener's emotions, despite looking simple on the page. This remarkable set of variations hides its beauties in just that way. It is based on a gracefully-stepping melody, which remains easily identifiable through five transformations of texture, rhythm and tonality.

Schumann's marking of *Ziemlich langsam* ('rather slow') gives a clue to the mood. The rising minor 7th (bars 1–2) is a key feature of the music, giving the music a yearning quality. When it returns, in the E major variation, but as a major 7th (bars 25–6), the beauty of this moment is almost unbearable. The phrase 'smiles behind the tears' is apt here. Other points of melodic genius include the triplets in the third variation: where the F♯ of bar 20 conveys hope, the equivalent note in bar 22 (F♮) is a cry of desolation. In the most moving performances a little rubato and sensitive tonal colouring will feature at these moments. A further opportunity for rhythmic flexibility comes in the fourth bar of the semiquaver variation; the music's flow seems to skip several heartbeats as the falling triads slow to a half-bar triplet. Time to reflect could be taken here, before returning to tempo in the next bar.

A touch of pedal to match each chord of the theme will add resonance to the tone, while still maintaining the important silences. The first three variations present the theme in soprano, then bass, and lastly alto voices; all will require careful balancing and tonal control. Especially when the left hand has the melody (second variation, beginning bar 13), musical shape and confident projection will be vital; the top line will also need focus here, but at a more reticent level. Pedalling in variations 1–4 should match harmonic changes, lifting as each chord is sounded and immediately replaced. In the semiquaver variation, pedal should be restricted to the note-lengths of the melody, so as not to cloud the carefully articulated accompaniment. Warm pedal would enhance the initial B major arpeggio in bar 37, but the penultimate bar might be left mostly unpedalled, to preserve the mood of this perfect miniature right to the end.

B:6 Turina *Duo sentimental*

The duo mentioned in the title can be thought of as flamenco singers – one male, one female – performing passionate poems of love and loss over luscious harmonies.

Exploration of these harmonies will alight on the many dominant 7th chords sliding in novel ways, or juxtaposed with augmented triads (e.g. bars 13–16). Especially colourful is the long passage over low pedal Cs, where chords on the flattened supertonic of D♭ major bring the popular music of the Iberian peninsula powerfully to mind.

Seemingly slender lines will need a true cantabile touch in order to find warmth and projection. For this singing tone, flexible forearm weight should be employed behind the hand. It may be helpful to imagine the fingertips clinging to each key, as if hanging off the edge of a cliff. A sensation of skin stuck by jam to the key surfaces often defines this feeling for students.

Only one passage presents fingering problems. At bars 28–33, the chords should be grouped in pairs and given legato fingering across the top of each pair. This will enable the semiquaver chords to flow smoothly to the following chord, for example (from the top) 5/4/2, then down to 4/2/1 over the bar-line 28–9. It is easy to miss the D♭s at the end of bars 28, 30 and 32, and in the repeat some bars later.

Marked dynamics are few – *piano* and quieter. This gives an intimate communication of the mood, but an expressive performance will be sensitive to detailed inflection of the melodic line. Surprise intervals, such as rising 7ths (e.g. bars 23–4) and even the mixed intervals of the left-hand melody in bars 7–12, need tonal awareness and musical shape. Testing the music's three main dynamic levels on the exam piano would be excellent use of the chance given to try out the piano before the exam starts; confidence about the level of *piano–pianissimo* available will allow a suitable opening level for this piece to be judged.

Subtle rubato will help melodies gain fluidity. Moments of special beauty can be lingered over, with counter-balancing flow forwards thereafter. Pedalling is relatively straightforward here – a certain amount of melodic smudging contributes to the atmosphere of sultry Spanish evening heat.

C:1 Harold Arlen and E. Y. Harburg
Over the Rainbow

Lovers of *The Wizard of Oz* or just this evergreen song will be delighted by Dave Stapleton's sensitive arrangement. For those unfamiliar with the music, a good starting-point is Judy Garland's delightfully innocent take on the song, after which the rather more expansive and mellifluous cover by Eva Cassidy may suggest an alternative mood.

The printed tempo of crotchet = *c*.72 allows the music to flow along gently but the injunction 'with rubato' suggests flexibility – if not to the extent of obscuring the pulse. Appropriate places for easing the tempo often occur at phrase-ends (for example bar 11 going into 12 and 20 into 21). Phrasing in general is an important aspect of performance, and singing through the melody, taking breaths every four bars, may help to achieve space and lyricism when playing; it will also make the interruption to the four-bar structure in bar 27 all the more telling. Your student could beneficially play the chords that fall on beat 3 of bars 8 and 24 more quietly than their neighbours, given that they are more harmonic than melodic in function.

There needs to be plenty of singing tone, so where the right hand has chords, the hand can be slightly tilted to the right in order for arm weight to be channelled down the outer fingers. Textures need to be supported by generous pedalling, and harmonic awareness will be crucial in determining where to clear the sound. Pedal changes are mostly by the minim but there are exceptions. In bars 13 and 17, for example, the pedal can be held down through the bar, but the last two beats of bar 10 and the first two of 11 will need to be separately pedalled. A fairly broad dynamic range is indicated and the opening *pianissimo* might benefit from use of the *una corda* pedal, but *forte* tone should retain a warm singing quality; achieving a good balance between right- and left-hand parts is therefore vital. As an alternative to the dynamics suggested in the score, a diminuendo through bar 27 and then a slight crescendo towards the end may also be effective.

This charmer is likely to be as welcome in a variety of concert settings as it will be in the exam room.

C:2 Villa-Lobos *Carangueijo (The Crab)*

This piece is based on a Brazilian children's song, but you don't have to be a child to enjoy its catchy rhythms. At first sight, three pages may seem on the long side – but by bar 28 virtually all the music has been disclosed, the remainder being mostly unvaried repetition.

One important performance feature that needs to be mastered is an effective left-hand staccato touch, which can be achieved via a crisp fingertip attack from a relaxed but firm wrist – the finger pulled rapidly upwards and slightly inwards immediately after striking the key. A controlled, very economical forearm rotation will also help. The chords at bar 21 etc. need strength, each the beneficiary of an incisive forearm drop starting an inch or two above the keyboard. Small hands can omit the lowest right-hand note without any great loss of power. Although much of the piece is quite loud, there are quieter moments too; these need to be played with the hands closer to the keys but with the same amount of articulative clarity as is required for the chordal playing.

The indicated tempo of crotchet = 120 yields a suitably lively pace, although a slower one (crotchet = c.112) will not lose the character. However, the pulse must be very stable, and so practising with a metronome (or with a reliable drummer!) will be beneficial. Where *rall.* is marked (bars 36 and 64), the difference in tempo can be quite substantial, in order to allow the sudden dynamic drop its full effect.

Overall, this is a fairly unproblematic piece for the grade, but to avoid a possibly monotonous military feel, it could be helpful to think of phrasing the principal melodic ideas as two bars, plus two bars, plus four bars – with dynamic nuancing incorporated accordingly. For example, a gentle emphasis on the downbeats of bars 6 and 8, later followed by one on the downbeat of bar 11, will help to outline the phrase structure, although overemphasis should be avoided if the performance is not to sound contrived.

The piece is by nature exuberant; it will suit the more extrovert among your students and could be a lively conclusion to the recital part of the exam.

C:3 Jian Zhong Wang *Long Deng Diao (Dragon Lantern Tune)*

This intriguing arrangement of a Chinese folksong is a good introduction to pentatonic-based melodies, albeit here spiced with foreign harmonies, with the regular presence of C♯ sometimes giving the music a Lydian feel.

If the downward arpeggiando effect (as indicated by directional arrows) is new to your students, a useful preparatory exercise is to sweep down any right-hand broken chord as fast as possible, sometimes holding on to the thumb note at the bottom of the chord. This could be practised at varying dynamic levels before transferring the technique back into the piece. In bars 23–4 and 61–2, the motion of passing the left hand gracefully over the right demands slow practice to establish a secure sense of keyboard geography.

The sustaining pedal does not need to be employed but its use will warm the textures in places such as bars 15–19 and much of bars 66–83, and its use will also help to join the low Ds in bar 95 with the final chord of the piece. The delicacy of the writing in bars 51–6 can be enhanced by applying the *una corda* pedal. Dynamic contrasts, as marked in the score, require some projection, although *forte* passages should not sound too harsh. Where dynamic levels vary between the hands, as with passages starting at bars 5 and 67, the left hand needs to be held close to the keys and as still as means allow, while the right hand and forearm will be more active, engaging a deeper touch.

The suggested tempo of minim = *c*.92 is fast and, with an instruction *Molto vivo*, the music must certainly move; however, a more moderate pace, down to minim = *c*.84, will achieve a similar effect. Adherence to a strict pulse is necessary (except where instructed otherwise) and care needs to be taken over the relative note-values so as to avoid compromising the tempo. Care should also be taken when the right hand plays dotted rhythms over left-hand triplets, the former's semiquaver being played fractionally after, not with, the latter's third quaver triplet.

This piece is a challenging option – but a very rewarding one!

C:4 Richard Rodney Bennett *Two Turtle-Doves*

Despite its picturesque title, this piece is also a study in right-hand 3rds. Therefore, fingerings should be adopted that will maximize connectivity by keeping the hand more-or-less in one position through a phrase. For example, opening the piece with right-hand fingering 5/2 then 3/1 keeps the hand-position fairly stable up to halfway through bar 4. This necessitates the use of 4/1 on the C/A♭ in bars 2 and 3, which is perfectly manageable if the hand is kept well forward on the keys. Since the 3rds presumably represent the two doves – one singing the upper part, the other the lower – a good legato is also appropriate in terms of imagery.

The metronome mark is quite slow (dotted crotchet = 54), making it important for a performance to avoid any feeling of six heavy beats per bar. This can be addressed by cultivating a gentle lilt in the playing, possibly even physically swaying to the music while practising (though probably not while performing!). The dynamic markings are mostly *mezzo-piano* and below, and even the single *forte* marking is qualified with *ma dolce*, so depth of touch and warmth are required here rather than force. The score instructs *una corda al fine*, yet caution is advisable. It is quite difficult to make a piano sing with the *una corda* pedal down, and *mezzo-forte/forte* levels can sound rather thin and hard if attempted through the muffler of the soft pedal. It may therefore only really be needed for the quietest sections.

The sustaining pedal, however, should be used throughout. According to context, it can be held unchanged through a bar until the final quaver (as in bars 1 and 2), or it can be changed on the beat (as in bars 5 and 7), or it can even be held through an entire bar (as in bars 20 and 22). Harmonic clarity is important, so both ear and foot need to be alert!

This piece comes from a set of twelve called *Partridge Pie* and its title refers to the well-known song 'The Twelve Days of Christmas'; it might therefore be suitable for inclusion in a seasonal concert.

C:5 Sofia Gubaidulina *Forest Musicians*

This fascinating miniature is an excellent introduction to the imaginative sound-world of the contemporary Russian composer Sofia Gubaidulina. The impression of space is an important textural feature, so the octave displacements indicated in the first bar should be noted.

Since rhythm is an important aspect of this music, the triplets, semiquavers and demisemiquavers need to be differentiated, especially where double-dotted rather than single-dotted rhythms are concerned. For example, beats 1–2 of bars 3 and 5 should not sound rhythmically the same. The suggested metronome mark of crotchet = 76 can be maintained throughout with no obvious need for any rubato. Dynamic contrasts also contribute to the music's character and these should be closely observed so that, for example, *forte* is used only once to emphasize the strident semitone in bar 17. Use of the *una corda* pedal will also be helpful at *pianissimo* levels. In bars 10–16 a slight adjustment to the dynamics may be desirable to aid clarity. If the left-hand cluster is played *pianissimo* and the right-hand notes *mezzo-piano*, any potential muddiness in the music may be avoided.

The fingering shown for the right-hand's note repetitions in bar 6 could also be helpfully applied to those in bar 36, given that fingers 3 and 2 are usually stronger than fingers 4 and 3. In bar 37, using the same finger for the repeated notes is an appropriate option, as long as the finger is kept close to the key and the hand as still as possible. In bars 5, 6, 27 and 29 the Ab minor chord, notated across two staves, can be taken in its entirety by the left hand, thus freeing the right for its delicate rhythmic work. This will also ensure that the full Ab minor harmony is still sounding when the pedal is released in bars 7 and 30. Adherence to the marked pedalling is advisable since the indications seem integral to the composer's musical effects.

This piece may not be to every student's taste, but it is worth exploring and fun can be had imagining just which 'forest musicians' are represented by the music.

C:6 Carl Vine *Threnody*

A threnody is a song of mourning, and here the title refers to 'all of the innocent victims' (of AIDS); it is little wonder that the music is filled with a profound bleakness.

At a first glance the three staves may seem off-putting but, once your student has worked out the keyboard layout of the first bar, the mystique begins to disappear because the same scheme is used throughout. Generally, the middle stave shows the most prominent melodic material, with the upper as a descant in ghostly harmonics; the lowest stave sketches out some slowly evolving harmonies, accompanied by precise, crucially important, pedal indications. The learning task may seem further eased by the fact that bars 17–24 are a repetition of bars 1–8.

Fingering and hand arrangements will need to be established in the very earliest stages of learning. Most of the middle-stave notes can be played comfortably by the left-hand thumb or index finger while finger 5 can reach down to the bass notes, perhaps changing to finger 2 when the notes in the lowest stave climb into the treble clef. Quavers in, for example, bars 2 and 4 can be judiciously divided between the hands. Although over-reliance on hands-separate practice can be counter-productive, practising the left-hand part on its own is probably necessary here, with the aim being to achieve an unhurried arm motion describing a series of graceful curves. Harmony notes (*piano*) can be lightly brushed, but crotchets in the middle stave need more projection (*mezzo-piano*). Here a moderate arm weight produced by the gentle motion of the left arm should provide the right speed of approach for the notes to ring out, bell-like, but without sounding over-forceful. The right hand (*ppp*) should be kept as close to the keys as possible, only lifting the fingers enough to ensure that the notes speak. A warm-up might involve practising a scale, gently swinging the left hand down into the keyboard while the right plays as quietly and motionlessly as possible.

The indicated tempo of crotchet = 54 yields an ideal tempo, one which generates a mood of sorrowful stillness and which also makes the kinaesthetic aspect not only manageable but central to the experience of the piece.

GRADE 7

The final grades should be equally rewarding not only to the students but also to the teachers and parents whose support and involvement in their development is so important. Grade 7 performances will usually sound enjoyable at pass level, while merit and distinction categories will acknowledge positive and assured performances showing real conviction and style. The highest marks most frequently go to candidates choosing pieces within their own technical comfort zone, so that expressive details and vivid communication really lift the music off the page.

A:1 Glinka *Fugue in A minor*

This relatively unknown piece may not seem at first sight the most obvious choice. However, a serious-minded student with a sufficiently keen eye and ear to unravel its contrapuntal twists and turns will be richly rewarded. The spirit of Bach never seems far away in this contemplative fugue, yet the chromaticisms and surprisingly bold gestures in the latter section place the piece firmly in the Romantic idiom.

The absence of dynamic markings before bar 58, with the exception of the occasional hairpin, provides scope for exploring one's own ideas. The predominantly thoughtful character seems to suggest warm, gentle tonal colours. At times, however, the three-voice texture pares down to two, creating a simpler, more airy feel; phrases that soar to a higher register benefit from a corresponding rise in dynamic level.

A measured yet flowing tempo will establish the thoughtful mood as voices enter in turn in the exposition. The upper of the two subjects at the opening, with its characteristic upward leaps, recurs throughout the fugue in various guises, including at one point in inversion. Marking each subject entry with a pen is a useful starting-point for understanding the counterpoint, as is playing each line of the three-voice texture either in isolation or in various combinations of lines.

Voicing the texture, perhaps the most important skill needed for this style, relies on an ability to put the spotlight on any part at will while subduing the others. Keen listening together with organized fingering will ensure that all notes are held for their full value, yet without ignoring the rests that provide punctuation to the phrasing. At times the line shifts between the hands, for instance in the tenor entry starting at bar 11, offering an extra challenge for the performer.

The mood of the piece seems set to continue throughout in much the same vein as the start until the organ-like left-hand octaves introduce grandeur and greater richness to the proceedings. The pedal, hitherto used sparingly (if at all), will help to sustain the harmonies as they progress towards the climax in the dominant in bar 62. Beginning the build-up as early as bar 53 works well, and arm weight will ensure a richness to the left-hand accents. The pause over the rest in bar 62 indicates release of the pedalled chord while the right-hand G♯ is held by the finger, producing an immediate decrease in tone in preparation for the five-bar ghostly hush which follows. The crescendo and slackening of pace at the Adagio bring the piece to an expansive, generously-toned close.

A:2 Handel *Sonatina in D minor*

This cheerful movement with its gigue-like rhythms and wealth of melodic interest has a spring in its step guaranteed to liven up any exam room.

Notes are fairly straightforward on the whole, although a few tricky corners might trip up the less well-prepared candidate – especially the continuous stream of right-hand quavers beginning at bar 14. Lightening offbeat quavers is the key to conveying that all-important four-in-a-bar buoyancy. That said, the relative simplicity of the opening must not lure students into setting an over-ambitious tempo which cannot be maintained. Each of the four cadential trills may be modified either to a three-note mordent beginning on the principal note, or to simply an upper grace note, if the suggested realization proves problematic.

Listening to or, better still, playing a harpsichord is an excellent starting-point for understanding the sound-world and how this piece might transfer to the piano. Clarity and brightness of attack are of paramount importance in this style. Ideally a mixture of detached and slurred notes will create rhythmic character but, as always, the teacher is the best judge of the extent to which each student is able to incorporate this detail while maintaining fluency. Slurring the first two quavers of each group of three will be effective for some bars – to highlight the melodic contours in bars 5–6, for instance.

It might be helpful to imagine the predominantly two-part texture played by two instruments, perhaps either violin and cello or oboe and bassoon. Although the melodic interest remains chiefly in the right hand, the occasional interplay between the hands, as in the opening bars, is a feature worthy of note. Matching the articulation is important here, especially the octave leaps which can be characterized by emphasizing the crotchet and lightly detaching the quaver. Rests, the importance of which is often overlooked, punctuate the phrases while also giving prominence to the crotchets.

At times all quavers assume equal melodic importance, for example at the opening, while elsewhere the first note of each three-quaver group has the main interest. Editorial dynamics, although not obligatory, offer a framework for conveying the structure. Bright, rather than heavy, *forte* tone maintains clarity of texture, and the echo effects, as if played on a two-manual harpsichord, will work well when the contrasts are made at exactly the right moment. In addition, gentle inflection of tone can mirror the undulations of the melodic line, for instance in bars 14–20 where the fall and subsequent rise in pitch suggest a diminuendo followed by a crescendo.

A:3 Mozart *Allegro*

If your student has never previously played a Mozart sonata, this wonderful movement with its combination of elegance and quasi-operatic drama is a perfect place to start.

The tempo, although Allegro, needs a spaciousness in order to convey the musical inflection and phrasing. Dynamics throughout are limited to *forte* and *piano*, and the musical context will dictate whether the changes are sudden, for dramatic effect, or more subtly integrated.

The opening section is dominated by a sense of movement towards the first beat, conveying either graceful gesture at the outset or drama and urgency at bar 16. The rests play an important role in adding definition to the phrasing and the semiquavers in bar 8 (which should 'flow like warm oil', in Mozart's own words) add an air of surprise and capriciousness to round off the phrase.

Dropping back in tone at bar 16 allows room for growth through the following bars. Light, detached octaves, using a hand touch, ensure that the right-hand semiquavers, which need reliable fingering, are not overpowered.

The second subject, which begins at bar 23, contains a wealth of musical ideas. Perfectly smooth right-hand suspensions at the start are answered by Scotch snaps, articulated in couplets. The semiquavers in bar 25 should be placed on, not before, the beat, and control of the left-hand accompaniment throughout the section will be aided by keeping the thumb close to the keys. Bars 27–30 embellish the subject; these bars rely on neat coordination of the hands and a stable pulse. The potentially troublesome thumb leap in bar 30 may need isolated practice. Dramatic contrasts abound in the bars that follow, with chromaticisms to be savoured and each of the three one-bar ideas seeming to increase in intensity. Trills may need to be modified, perhaps even to four-semiquaver turns, in order not to prevent a scramble through bars 43–4.

Surely one of the loveliest moments of the movement occurs at bar 45. Here sensitive right-hand voicing and well-planned fingering will allow clarity to the suspensions before the music heads purposefully towards the double bar.

The leaner texture and seemingly more relaxed pacing at the start of the short development section create a welcome moment of reflection. Rests let in the air and the left-hand 3rds should not be allowed to dominate the texture. The quavers then propel the movement forward towards the recapitulation, which contains many similar musical challenges to those encountered thus far. Crisply articulated staccatos provide energy and excitement but, as elsewhere, the music's natural poise and grace must not be compromised by rushing.

A:4 J. S. Bach *Allemande*

This wonderful dance movement, with its clear structure and strong harmonic foundation, is suitable for a confident player who will be able to manage safely the twists and turns of the musical line as it switches between treble and bass.

Plenty of practice hands-separately, perhaps initially legato, will ensure that both hands are equally secure; smooth thumb movements, anticipating each new position, will be the key to a seamless musical line. Coordination between the hands becomes trickier when the left hand plays semiquavers, especially in the second half, with particular care needed when the right hand moves after a tie.

Despite the somewhat busy look of the piece, the Allemande tempo needs a spaciousness and poise throughout. Ornaments serve to enhance the melodic line, but, as always, an over-intricate realization may compromise the musical flow. Listening to Bach's unaccompanied violin partitas will provide some clues to phrasing the string-like figuration. Further understanding of the texture can be gained by imagining the movement played as a violin and cello duet.

Ideally a mixture of slurred and detached semiquavers, using either a finger or light-hand touch, will produce the most stylish effect. However, phrasing choices are of course dictated to an extent by each individual student's ability (and patience!). Some initial work combining these two phrasing elements, perhaps using a five-finger exercise or scale, will help to develop the quickness of finger response needed for true clarity.

Looking beyond the intricacy of the figuration reveals the underlying harmonies; the speed of harmonic change generally alternates between crotchets and minims. The first half of the binary structure may be divided into three arching phrases of approximately four bars, each of which dovetails neatly with its neighbour. A natural rise and fall in tone is implied in each phrase, and the sequences that occur in both halves offer scope for some dynamic terracing. Syncopations in bars 9–10 add yet further musical interest. The momentary hint of C♯ minor at the end of bar 4 indicates a turning-point after which the tonality settles on B major, yet with occasional A♮s.

Many of the same features recur in the second half, during which the return back to the home key is reached via a series of modulations. However, the offbeat left-hand notes which anticipate bars 15 and 16 are a feature worthy of highlighting, and a phrasing decision will be needed for the right-hand patterns in bars 20–2 while the other hand articulates its semiquavers.

A:5 J. S. Bach, trans. Alkan *Siciliano*

The inclusion of this lovely transcription of the second movement of the Sonata in E flat for flute and keyboard reflects the current renewed interest in this genre among pianists. Its lyrical character and leisurely two-in-a-bar siciliano rhythms seem to embrace both Baroque and Romantic styles, making it an ideal and refreshingly different choice for a sensitive student.

Combining the flute and keyboard parts creates an intricate texture that does not always lie easily under the hands. Skilful fingering is needed to maintain legato wherever possible, especially when both right-hand notes move in semiquavers, as in bars 13 and 15, and a keen eye will make sure that leger lines are not misread.

Tracing the flute line throughout the piece, or better still, listening to the piece in its original form, will provide the key to understanding the texture.

A sensitive ear and plenty of imagination are required for translating the clarity of flute tone into a rich yet gentle cantabile on the piano. The harmonic framework is underpinned by the bass notes, often marked *ten.* (tenuto) for added prominence, over which the semiquaver patterns add rhythmic lilt and momentum.

Good control of the inner notes as they switch between the hands will ensure that they do not become confused with the melodic notes, especially when they share the same register. Pedalling needs selective use throughout, in order to convey not only the richness but also the clarity of the texture. For example, bars 6–7 require changes every quaver and the scalic runs may be better left unpedalled.

Playing the semiquavers alone will reveal that, in addition to filling out and elaborating the harmonies, they also assume a more melodic role at times. Making the most of the *pianissimo* will highlight the echo at bar 9, and the restatement of the opening phrase can be coaxed by a momentary slight easing of the tempo. Increasing dynamic level at this point, albeit within the context of the overall gentle mood, will convey the brighter mood suggested by the change to major. The more intricate texture at bar 13 calls for sensitively shaped semiquavers and four bars later the imitation conveys a hint of agitation. A subtle transition as the music slips back into the home key for the final statement of the opening idea needs just as subtle shaping and pacing of the semiquavers. Finally, gracefully shaded appoggiaturas, with both notes equally spaced, together with the diminished 7th harmony in the penultimate bar, adds a further touch of beauty to the ending.

A:6 D. Scarlatti *Sonata in A*

This lively sonata, best suited to a confident student with the agility to cope with its fast-moving technical challenges, seems to reflect the sunny Mediterranean climate of this composer's homeland. It is packed with quirky musical ideas and forms an excellent introduction to Scarlatti's characterful style.

The relatively straightforward opening may tempt candidates to set off at a pace that cannot be comfortably maintained. Although it needs a one-in-a-bar energy, the tempo choice is governed largely by the wide leaps and rapid hand-crossing.

Phrasing of the quavers throughout the piece presents various options. While a detached touch gives buoyancy and energy to the rhythm, some slurs might also be incorporated for variety, especially from the first to second quavers of the bar. Rapid semiquavers, distributed between the hands, are a common feature of the composer's writing; they will need an athlete's quickness of response in order to prevent unevenness of tone or pacing. Memorizing the jumps, spotting the new position in advance of playing, is the key to accuracy. Practising these moves, while adding a further octave distance to the leap, may help to develop lateral freedom and confidence required over the keyboard. Hand distribution in bars 15–17, and elsewhere, needs careful planning in order to facilitate the upward leaps. One option at this point is to split the G♯ and A at the bar-line between the hands, playing the second note with the left hand.

Although the ornaments are integral to the style, rhythmic momentum must not be disturbed by trying to fit in too many notes. For instance, the trill in bar 19 may be played as a mordent and, if proving problematic, those in bars 67–74 can be modified to become acciaccaturas.

The harpsichord style calls for a crisp, incisive touch. Dynamic decisions are largely determined by the constantly changing moods. The repetition of the opening five-bar phrase offers scope for the first of many echoes, an effect particularly suited to a two-manual instrument. The unexpectedly bold flamenco-like guitar chords at bar 29 evoke the music of Spain and Portugal where Scarlatti worked for much of his life. Convention is broken by ending each half of the binary structure in the minor key, and the earlier modulation to D minor at bar 17 (remembering the C♯s in bars 18 and 20) also appears as a surprise. A crescendo through bars 67–79 works well, as the left-hand patterns seem to gather momentum, while the more sustained texture with its tied notes that follows suggests a more peaceful mood.

B:1 Mingxin Du and Zuqiang Wu *Shui Cao Wu (The Dance of Watergrass)*

If your students enjoy playing something out of the ordinary, this may be the very piece for them. In order to appreciate this alternative sound-world it may help to look at the delicacy and detail of some Chinese paintings – easily found online.

The tempo is not fast, and the suggested metronome speeds work well. Although the piece appears lengthy, it has quite a lot of repetition, and the rippling left-hand accompaniment is not at all difficult once a suitable fingering is established. The eight-bar introduction creates a peaceful atmosphere, conjuring up a scene by the lake or seashore. Pedal need only be changed every two bars at first, and then with the moving bass octaves. Thereafter, a regular pedal change on the first beat of each bar is all that is needed, except for a handful of bars in the middle section. In bars 36–8 and 41–6, some players may prefer to change on first and third beats for the sake of clarity.

The movement of weeds or grasses underwater is beautifully portrayed by the repetitive left-hand figures, and as they are played the hand and arm will sway from side to side. Apart from a leap from the first semiquaver in a few bars, most of the notes lie within reach if the suggested fingering is adopted. The choice of finger for the fourth semiquaver in each bar will depend on the individual player: some may be happy with the fourth finger; others may prefer to use the third or even the second. Whichever is chosen, the repeated notes in the middle of the pattern (in bars 9–12 it is F♯) act as a pivot around which the other notes revolve.

In the right hand, swaying spread chords are answered by swirling semiquaver figures, often high in the treble. As they begin to drift downwards (from bar 21) every effort should be made to glide smoothly, avoiding a bump on first-beat chords. As the music subsides, the key changes to B minor (bar 29), preparing the way for the middle section. It is important to observe the *tranquillo* here, because the offbeat rhythm employed between the hands is often used to express agitation, and clearly this is not what the composer wants. The left hand, marked *piano*, has the melody and only needs the slightest rise and fall in tone to outline its arch-like shapes. The right-hand chords shadow the melody and must be kept *pianissimo* until a strong crescendo and ritenuto at bar 50 herald the return of the principal theme.

B:2 MacDowell *By a Meadow Brook*

Edward MacDowell is probably best known for his charming miniature 'To a Wild Rose', another of the *Woodland Sketches*. 'By a Meadow Brook' is very different in character and will provide the pianist with plenty of challenges, both musical and technical.

The brook is very active. Sometimes it ripples or frolics; sometimes it cascades or becomes boisterous; only occasionally is it peaceful. It could easily be the setting for Shakespeare's *A Midsummer Night's Dream*, with the fairies playing by moonlight and Puck up to mischief.

Performers differ widely in the tempo they choose for this piece, ranging from dotted minim = 63 as printed in the score to a more relaxed speed of about dotted minim = *c.*52 as suggested in the footnote. The graceful, merry character can be achieved at a slower tempo as long as the necessary lightness and sparkle are present; speed is almost never the most important factor in a performance. It will be important to gradually build a reliable and fluent right hand. The arm must move freely to allow the fingers to negotiate the rippling triplet figures cleanly, and a reliable fingering that suits the player is a prerequisite. Your student needs to look out for the D♭ in bar 14 – it could easily be missed.

The left hand plays a supporting role for most of the time, albeit a very important one. Practising it with the pedal will be useful, changing with the harmony but always observing staccato chords when they occur. Very little pedal is needed in the middle section. There could be a touch on the dotted crotchet C♯ in bar 22 and on the minim chords in bars 27 and 29–31. Bearing in mind the eventual speed, the trills in bars 17, 19 and 21 will be quite acceptable as semiquavers. If each trill is stopped on the second half of the third beat there will be time to prepare for the next bar. For those who are more ambitious the trill could be in triplet semiquavers, but demisemiquavers might be a step too far!

The composer has provided plenty of dynamics, but many of the hairpins are merely nuances and should not be overdone. At bar 6 the volume may have increased to about *mezzo-forte* before dropping back to *piano* in bar 11. Only in the middle section is there any loud playing. The *una corda* pedal could be used to control the tone in bars 17–20, but is certainly needed from bar 47 to the end as the scene fades and the merry-makers disappear into thin air.

B:3 Palmgren *Kevätyö (Night in May)*

Selim Palmgren was nicknamed the 'Finnish Chopin'; like his contemporary and compatriot Sibelius, many of his compositions were inspired by nature. This tender, evocative description of a May night will appeal to the student with imagination and an ear for subtle shades of tone. It is essentially a love song but one that is only whispered into the scented night air.

Dynamics rarely rise above *pianissimo*; just one phrase is marked *poco cresc.*, and it quickly falls back again. The last section is marked *ppp* and ends *pppp*, so it would not be unreasonable to employ the *una corda* pedal throughout. The only real challenge is to negotiate accurately the three or four phrases that have a lot of accidentals. Success will depend on discovering how the chord progressions are constructed (how to crack the code!) and on the hands' learning of the shapes to be able to feel their way across the keyboard. The minim B at the top of the spread chord in bar 22 can most easily be played with the right hand.

If the right-hand chords in bar 7, for instance, are looked at without the second note from the top, they are immediately seen as a progression of first inversion minor triads descending in whole-tone steps. If first practised like this using fingers 1/2/5, it will be easy to add the third finger a tone above the second finger later. In bars 13 and 15 all notes are played on the white keys, and this figure, marked *misterioso*, should drift like the softest of breezes. Then at bar 21 the top notes move down chromatically above pairs of 3rds; the first and last pair are minor 3rds, the others major. Your students should be encouraged to make these discoveries for themselves.

The sustaining pedal will be needed throughout the piece, changing only as the harmony changes or where melody notes move consecutively as in bars 1 and 3. Here a change midway on the lowest note should be all that is needed. If the chords are played quietly enough it will be effective to hold the pedal right through bars 12–13, and again through bar 15. It is as though the chords are just floating on a wash of sound. Following bars where there have been several accidentals there is a danger that those of the key signature are forgotten – the G♯s in bar 11 and F♯s in bars 17–18, for instance.

With the challenges solved, the player should relax and enjoy the atmospheric beauty of the music.

B:4 Cui *Waltz*

César Cui is the least known of the group of Russian composers called the 'Mighty Handful'. Rimsky-Korsakov, Borodin and Mussorgsky are by far the more familiar names, but this beautiful waltz by Cui deserves to be heard.

The whole piece is built out of a yearning three-note figure, its appoggiatura first rising and later falling (from bar 17). The texture consists of three layers: the principal melody at the top, a supporting bass melody, and an inner accompaniment that is divided between the hands. As a first step, it would be worthwhile practising just the melody and bass line together without the aid of pedal. This will train the ear to listen for the correct balance of these two voices. Next, the left hand and pedal should be practised, holding the first note in each bar so that it is caught as the pedal change is made. Any notes that are part of the inner accompaniment must be quieter, of course.

Many players, especially those with a limited stretch, will find it easier to play the rising melody notes with the fifth finger: the fourth finger on the B♯ in bar 2 in the recommended edition makes the leap down to A♯ even wider. Where the motif falls, at bar 18 and similar, the fingering in this edition is more practical. In bar 26 it would be easier to play the dotted minim E with the left hand. Wide intervals and overlapping parts make bars 33–4 rather awkward. If preferred, it would be possible to take all the F♮s with the left hand and the A (second beat of bar 34) with the right.

A significant feature of the middle section (starting at bar 27) is the C pedal note in the bass. It will be important to observe the ties, securely holding this note when the pedal is changed. Pedalling is clearly marked except at the most dramatic passage (bars 44–9) when the music urges forward with a sudden crescendo. All the notes belong to one chord, a dominant minor 9th, so with the low B underpinning the texture, the pedal should be held right through until the dotted crotchet in bar 49. This note should be held long enough for its tone to subside before resuming the dance.

A swaying one-in-a-bar will sweep the music along and conjure up the atmosphere of a haunted ballroom. With the coda, from bar 77, the music begins to fade, and the *una corda* pedal will help to capture the scene as the dancers drift away.

B:5 Liszt *Piano Piece No. 2*

There could hardly be a better introduction to the piano music of Franz Liszt than this beautiful miniature. However, care will be needed in the initial note-learning stage.

The use of chromatic harmony, unusual chord progressions and enharmonic changes results in many unexpected accidentals. It might be helpful to label the basic chords. For instance, the first phrase consists of two bars using the tonic chord, followed by two bars of F♯ minor, and one bar of A major, with the last four back in the tonic again. Other chords, the so-called colour chords, may not be so easily named by your student – especially as suspensions and appoggiaturas abound – but at all times the key signature must be remembered if wrong notes are to be avoided.

Most of the pedalling will go from one bass note to the next regardless of its note-value, and at bar 15 (where the music settles into the key of G♭

major) the pedal should not be changed until arriving at the C♭ in bar 18. In bar 40 a half-pedal will give clarity to the change of chord in the left hand. Then after the two-beat silence there will be no need to change the pedal through the rising octaves if a positive crescendo is made. Judicious use of half-pedalling in bar 48 will allow something of the previous bass-note C♮ and the harmony to remain until the new chord in bar 49. At the final cadence, a magical effect may be achieved by delaying the pedal change for the last chord until the top note has been reached. Success will depend on counting carefully and listening closely as the semibreve chord fades (*smorzando*) and the spread chord begins. The *una corda* pedal will help.

The dynamic colour and rubato needed is far greater than indicated in the score. With each unexpected harmony, every curve in the melody or change of mood the pianist must respond with subtle nuances or dramatic contrast. The climax of the first half is reached at bar 15, but when the melody is repeated (bar 20) it is suddenly tender, and the octave A♭ should be held and relished. The mood changes with the first appearance of a diminished 7th chord, in bar 27, becoming restless and urgent. The gradual crescendo has to be carefully judged, and with it the music seems to press forward until broadening as the massive climax is reached in bar 39. The return to A♭ major (bar 43) heralds a valedictory declaration which eventually subsides into silence.

B:6 Mendelssohn *Gondellied (Allegretto non troppo)*

Mendelssohn was a great traveller; he spent ten happy and productive months in Italy, inspired by the music and landscape of that country. Although this particular gondola song is not included in the *Songs without Words*, it shares a similar character with the three that are. It is possible that Mendelssohn had intended composing another set. Whatever the background may be, this appealing boat song is well worth learning.

After the short introduction, where the left hand plays the bass line and the right hand the accompaniment, the left hand has to take on both roles. This involves moving quickly and smoothly over quite a wide range of notes. Plenty of time should be given to practising the left hand and pedal together before attempting to add the right hand. For much of the piece the pedal need only be changed on first beats. Occasionally it is possible to pedal through two bars: in bars 1–2 (where the harmony is static); bars 7–8 and similar (where the melody consists of notes of the same chord); and bars 44–5 and 48–9 (where the melody ascends). However, changing the pedal halfway through a bar is sometimes necessary. This will be the case in bars 3–4 and 50–1 where the bass line descends stepwise, and bars 11–12 (and similar) where the right hand has several changes of harmony. Success in pedalling depends on the amount of tone employed, on the use of nuances and balance of the hands, and, above all, on listening at all times.

Mendelssohn was very fond of doubling his melodies so that they move in 3rds or 6ths – an idea borrowed from Italian opera. It would help to imagine this sung by two voices or played on a pair of woodwind instruments. At bar 7, the melody should enter at a *mezzo-forte* level (some editions do not have a dynamic mark here), in order to create room for the diminuendo that follows. The middle section (bars 23–34) builds to a powerful climax in C major where the pedal could be held down for fully three bars, until the sudden change to *piano* in bar 33.

The tempo should flow gently, two in a bar, to suggest the rocking movement of the gondola. Much of the final section is quiet, and *una corda* pedal will add atmosphere to those bars marked *pianissimo*. One can imagine standing on a bridge in Venice as the gondola passes beneath and makes its way down the canal, the song of the gondolier gradually fading in the distance.

C:1 Sylvie Bodorová *Carousel*

Performers who like to show off both their imagination and virtuosity have a treat in store with this addictive whirling, merry-go-round of a piece. Better still, it's not as hard as it might seem.

The foundation work will be crucial – in the hands of an impatient learner, the piece may fall apart under pressure. It needs conscientious, thoughtful preparation of the notes – careful fingering and counting, and practising the musical detail at a slow tempo. Particularly important is an accurate transition from the dotted crotchets to crotchets; the quaver pulse must remain absolutely constant, and the tenuto marks very much dictate that each beat is given its full length.

Thereafter the ability to play at speed will come, but the instruction 'as fast as possible' does not mean 'faster than possible' or 'faster than appropriate'. The eventual tempo should be no quicker than one that allows shape, detail, articulation and rhythmic clarity. This will depend on the piano and the performer but dotted crotchet = 150 would work well. The opening might be the best guide as to tempo, since the crisp articulation of the quavers with a subtle combination of finger and wrist staccato close to the keys needs to be comfortable and controlled.

A small comma just after the crescendo in bar 39 will enhance the *subito piano* for the easier-looking quavers of the middle section as the carousel whirls around. This is, however, one of the harder sections as hands need to jump with effortless accuracy and control. Slow practice is beneficial here, using the time the hands are not playing to cover instantly and prepare the next notes while working at a smooth crescendo to the climax in bar 56. This *sforzando* must be dramatic but still within the context of the overall dynamic. Almost all instances of *sforzando* should be given a dab of direct pedal to avoid harshness, and this might also be applied to the tenuto chords. Dynamics throughout should be clearly communicated.

Bars 77–80 need to be well controlled; right-hand work may be needed here to balance the chords to the top and give stability, though there is no harm in an excited performance having a small, momentum-gathering accelerando towards the glorious glissando. Using the thumb, your student can take time over the last two bars, judging the finger's angle and firmness so that the nail comes to rest against the side of each note – otherwise the drama of the final octave may be more about a painful burn than a virtuosic flourish.

C:2 Debussy *Canope*

The beauty and mystery of this haunting prelude quickly transcend any of the rather gory associations that this city of ancient Egypt has. The music couples evocative images of unknown antiquity and stories of a long-forgotten past with Debussy's unique harmonic world.

While the important foundation work in most pieces lies in the fingering and slow technical work, here the better place to start is with images and sounds. The challenges are not so much in playing the notes themselves, but in doing so with nuance, balance, colour and tonal subtlety. Your student needs first to have the sounds of a particular interpretation in mind, and then to strive to achieve them technically. Just how should the opening chords be voiced, for instance? To the top, balanced, or to the outside octaves? How might the opening be shaped? To the final chord, to the first chord of bar 2, or to be presented still and unruffled?

The dynamic range only extends from *pianissimo* to *piano*, so it is best to consider how comfortably a *pianissimo* can be controlled and judge the overall dynamic breadth from there. Since the range could be a little broader than the markings suggest, it is imperative to try out the piano before any performance.

Debussy's abundant musical detail all adds to the effectiveness of the performance. The *cédez* in bar 4, for example, should beguile the listener and enhance the unheralded frisson of the D minor chord; the *piano* tenuto A of bar 7 needs to have just enough tone to rise above the enveloping *pianissimo* chord, allowing the chromatic melody to weave its enigmatic character over the top. In bars 11–14 the harmonies need to be warm and sustained but the delicate melodic line should penetrate through the texture without much blurring from the pedal; the fingers therefore need to hold the chords as much as possible. In bars 14–16 some thought will be needed as to which lines and notes to bring to the front of the texture.

All this needs to happen within a relaxed, broad, yet strongly felt underlying pulse, with the rubato never too distorted and with a subtle awareness of pedal – which Debussy implies rather than notates. Grace notes should be light and gently tucked-in, and a sense of urgency and tension within the *animez* should be avoided, simply allowing a gentle flow forwards. Important moments such as the reprise in bar 26 should be communicated with a generous pause, the performance then slowing to the intensely subtle and expressive final phrase, poignant over its comforting bed of C major harmony.

C:3 Shostakovich *Prelude in D flat*

This delightful quirky piece, which evokes images of a silent comedy, is at first a grotesque waltz. However, its chromatic opening and rather darkly comic middle section eventually give way to a wonderfully jubilant reprise of the opening firmly in D♭ major. Empathy with an understanding of the piece's character are needed for it to have joy and enthusiasm in performance; it will be a fabulous addition to a student's repertoire.

The piece is typically Shostakovich in its chromatic harmonies and the sparsity of its piano texture, so attention to detail and precise foundation work are needed; there is little to hide behind if the hands don't know their way around this piece flawlessly. Crucial in achieving this, and reaping huge rewards, will be consistent fingering with the appropriate articulation, dynamic and balance, all of it given slow but musical repetition; your student in effect learns the piece from memory but has the score there as an aide-mémoire.

Initially the jokey melodic line is primarily in the left hand; since listeners are naturally drawn to higher registers, balance needs to be carefully judged to prevent the right-hand accompaniment obscuring the lower melodic line. The diminuendo in bar 3 should therefore be taken literally, with the upbeats kept even lighter to allow the left hand to take charge of the storyline from the very first note.

A neatness and precision in the staccato will bring out the personality – but with variety in the articulation to highlight the humour. A slightly longer staccato on the first few notes – for instance, lightening and shortening as the melody rises – will give more character and shape. The piece's dance-like feel would be lost if too much rubato were used, yet a small amount of it will add to the piece's attractiveness.

Despite the prevalence of musical detail, Shostakovich gives little indication of the phrasing. Some thought needs to go into this to avoid a rather breathless approach. A little lift in bars 8, 16, 24 etc. is worth considering to give the line more obvious shape and direction, and dynamic shading will enhance the melody.

The adventurous student could try Shostakovich's ambitious metronome marking, but a slower dotted minim = *c*.69 will still allow a brisk one-in-a-bar lilt; indeed, a fairly wide tempo range will work as long as the performance has momentum, the fingers find their way securely and musically, and the dynamic markings are convincingly conveyed. The boldest sound must be saved for the joyous *fortissimo* at bar 42, and the cheeky surprise ending should be enjoyed – a confident yet subtle *pianissimo* bringing a light-hearted smile to the music.

C:4 Dichler *Toccata-Etüde*

The daunting title may deter some, but Prokofiev this is not, and the 'moderato' in the tempo marking should be borne in mind. A charming and cheerful dance-like piece, perhaps revealing Dichler's Viennese roots, it presents only modest technical demands for a pianist who has good co-ordination – and of its 39 bars there are only 28 to learn.

Essential to a convincing performance is the rhythmic and tonal control of the chords in the outer sections. Since it could easily become heavy and cumbersome, bright voicing to the top of each hand and a lively staccato touch in the fingers from a light wrist staccato will help the rhythmic excitement and clarity. Hands need to find their way to the next chord with confidence, so careful and consistent fingering is required and shadow jumping ahead of the pulse will promote fluency. Little pedal is needed except to warm the first beats.

Different challenges are presented by the middle section, which is – effectively – two four-bar phrases, each closing with a ritardando. Both phrases need an eloquent, singing melodic line over the opening rhythmic motif, which now has a much more lyrical quality to its articulation. The relaxation of the tempo is important here; there is also a warmer and more generous use of pedal, even during the semi-staccato quaver arpeggio. Focusing listening on the long melodic notes will help in assessing the balance – particularly through the dotted minim which needs to be omnipresent for its duration rather than swallowed by the accompaniment.

Dynamically, some decisions need to be made. What appears to be a constant diminuendo for the final 13 bars has to be graded carefully. There needs to be a good, strong crescendo in bar 26, and much should be made of the hairpins to keep the excitement going, both here and in the opening figures.

A little playfulness with the pulse will help the dance-like feel; for instance, a fraction of time at the end of the first bar will prepare an elegant placing of the first beat of the second bar. The tempo needs consideration too. On a good, bright piano the faster end of the suggested tempo range might be possible, but given that clarity is much more important than speed it will be advisable, on most instruments, to proceed at a more measured tempo with good precision and articulation, and being particularly aware of the final few bars as the pitch descends. While slowing down as marked, your student must keep the articulation transparent to prevent the performance becoming too muddy, before the final low C and delightful *ppp* chord.

C:5 M. Gould *China Blue*

For those who like something a little different this is a remarkable, ravishing and teasing piece. It is a pentatonic Chinese cocktail with a hint of the blues, a twist of the contemporary, and a backdrop of downtown New York City. With its seductively simple opening, it looks predictable on the page. However, it will require a fair amount of educating into the fingers.

Preparation should begin by planning intelligent fingering and writing it in; there is otherwise the possibility of inconsistency from practice to practice, given the many fingering options. It needs to be organized in such a way that the 4ths, for instance, can be performed as legato as possible, particularly across the top line; this will enable the pedal to be subtly changed without disjointing the melody.

The opening immediately conjures up the mood; a relaxed, straight-eight tempo is needed, coupled with some subtle pedalling. Your student should avoid taking the marking too literally, instead adjusting to the room and the instrument, sustaining the pedal beyond the bracket with a slow, misty lift before the rests. Subtle dynamic shading will also help set up the atmosphere before the right hand enters.

Small details will enhance the performance. The accented chords are abrupt interventions, almost rock-like in their impetus, and the grace notes should be tucked tightly into, and almost together with, the chords. Playing them first at exactly the same time as the 4ths and then fractionally separating them will lead to the right effect. The tremolandos will work well if begun as a chord and then shaken out of the hand – and in bar 19, with its acciaccatura, having the three notes sound as a chord before starting the tremolando gives a much stronger first beat and a rich sonority.

Underneath these tremolandos the left hand has some challenging jumps, which should be practised without pedal. Watching the hand travel to the notes will help ensure that the distance is carefully ingrained into the physical memory; practising with eyes closed is also helpful.

Bars 26 and 27 are particularly awkward, needing some conscientious shadow jumping of the left hand; another tactic is to play the left-hand chords in time with the previous right-hand quaver to encourage the hand to jump quickly. The articulation here should be interpreted literally, the suggested emphases implying a crescendo through to the accented chords and setting up a strong dynamic before the long diminuendo. This should be a gentle and subtle fading-away with plenty of pedalled sonority until the lonely, exposed final bar.

C:6 Peter Sculthorpe *1st movt: from Sonatina*

This is a dramatic, intensely evocative piece, and a gem for musically imaginative, intelligent and inquisitive performers. It has atmosphere and drama in its sonorous use of the full range of the instrument, excitement in the middle section's rhythmic energy and tension, and a thrilling, virtuosic climax before the haunting opening returns.

There should be thoughtful, musical planning at the beginning of the learning journey. The piece needs careful fingering, and slow and detailed observation of the rhythms, articulation and score – taking a small section (perhaps no more than two bars) at a time. Virtually every note has some musical marking and requires careful consideration, in order to ensure that the sounds are established in the mind, ear and fingers. None of it is hard if given enough care and slow, accurate, musical repetition.

The *8va bassa* of the atmospheric opening ten bars, with all left-hand notes an octave lower, gives a wonderful, deep cavernous sound. The pedal should be carefully placed to link the bass to the undulating chords. These chords should be shaped to the first beat of the bar and balanced to the top. Bars 5 and 6 are bell-like in their abruptness; the diminuendo is an echo as the sound rings around the landscape. Bars 9 and 10 are hard to read but easy once the notes and rhythm are internalized; immediately learning them from memory is therefore advisable.

The middle section needs to be rhythmic, clear (*senza Ped.*) and neatly articulate: the left hand to the fore initially; the right hand prominent through the crescendo and rallentando until the abrupt return to tempo in bar 25 with the intensity and tension of the chromatic melody. There are some short sprints and moments of recovery before exhaustion sets in during bars 39–48.

The large final section is a brooding and frightening climax, again without pedal but carefully controlled in its crescendo, within which the phrase-markings serve to indicate a dynamic shape, not a legato. The rallentando can be used to achieve greater sonority in the octaves – the length of the dramatic low Cs stretched slightly and the rests enhanced both for effect and to ensure that the left hand can travel the leaps to the next notes.

The return to the calmer opening should be abrupt and surprising, noticing the accent on the first left-hand C as it will need to penetrate the texture and tone of the *fortissimo* chord. Lots of time and space should be allowed in the final bars, and the pedal held at the double bar for the fate-resigned *pausa lunga.*